BLUEJACKET

A SAILOR'S LIFE

CHET BRIGHT
with
DEREK TURNER

Dedicated to all the present-day Navy SEALs and EOD specialists who continue the good work began during World War II.

BLUEJACKET
(bloo-jak-it)
noun
An enlisted person in the U.S. or British navy; a sailor

"Chet Bright is a deep-diving, double-crimping,
steely-eyed frogman, a bare-knuckle fighter,
sailor of sailors and the last of the ballroom dancers.
Be prepared to read an exciting adventure that leaves you with envy,
laughter and sadness. Thoroughly enjoyable.
A must read for all."

– Capt. James R. Lake, U.S. Navy (Retired)
EOD/UDT/SEAL, BUDS Class 55,
former commander of Explosive Ordnance Disposal Mobile Unit 3
and Naval School Explosive Ordnance Disposal

PART ONE

PROLOGUE

I didn't bring my toothbrush or a comb for my hair. No extra set of clothes or pair of socks, not even a sack lunch. I did bring my schoolbooks. I had to bring those. Otherwise, they'd know.

I walked out the door that morning like any other, and stole a last glance over my shoulder at the tiny rental house we'd moved into months earlier when my father brought us to this dusty place where he'd found work. I walked toward Fort Davis High School, where I'd recently began my senior year, but when I got there, I kept walking. I wasn't going to school.

Pecos, Texas, that's where I was going.

It was about seventy-five miles to the north and if that thumb I had in the air couldn't persuade someone to stop, it was going to be a hell of a long walk. I kept on.

The two-lane highway stretched out in front of me. I fixed my eyes on the horizon, but I aimed to go much farther than that. When a man in a passing car took pity on me and pulled onto the shoulder, I jogged up to the passenger door, opened it and climbed inside.

"Where you headed?" the man asked.

"Pecos," I said.

That was about the extent of our conversation. He didn't ask what a teenage boy was doing thumbing down the road or what exactly was in Pecos. He only told me he wasn't going that far. I told him I'd be obliged if he took me as far as he was going. And he did. I thanked him for that.

I spent the rest of the day kicking rocks along the side of the road and waiting for the next kind soul. I'd covered about thirty-five miles, not quite halfway there, when another car stopped for me in Balmorhea. This guy wasn't going to Pecos, either. He was going back to Fort Davis and something about the star on his chest and the "Jeff Davis County Sheriff" stenciled on the side of the car told me I was going with him.

My little adventure had come to a premature end, but if I'm being honest, I was almost glad of it. I was tired and I was hungry and I maybe should have planned it all a little better.

The drive back home passed in silence, but that silence was broken when I walked through the front door.

My mother erupted in a fierce mixture of relief and anger, the sort of combination only a mother can conjure up when she realizes that her child has done something stupid but managed to luck his way through it unharmed. She'd been worried sick, she told me, and how could I run off like that?

My father stood and stared while my mother ranted and raved. That's how he was. He preferred working to talking, but we always knew what he'd say, so usually he didn't bother. When my mother had exhausted everything on her mind, his message was brief.

"Chet, you need to think this through," he said.

The trouble was, I had thought it through. I'd thought about it until my head hurt every day for the last ten months. I'd been bugging my parents to let me go ever since the voice on the radio told us what happened. The president of the United States called it a day that will live in infamy, and I knew that he was right.

I was sixteen years old when the Japanese bombed Pearl Harbor. I'd had some vague knowledge about foreign armies fighting each other on the other side of the world, but until December 7, 1941, my future, as I saw it, certainly included nothing more adventurous than a lifetime of sweating in the oil fields of West Texas.

Now I knew just as surely that we were at war and that the war could not be won without my help. I just had to get out there and get some of those dirty, rotten Japs.

That's why I was going to Pecos that fall day in 1942. I'd turned seventeen on September 13, but I was going to tell the recruiter there that I was eighteen, only a small lie, and that I was ready to fight.

I had played it out in my head a thousand times. I was going to win the whole damn war singlehanded. There was nothing that could stand in my way.

Well, almost nothing. There was the small matter of Charley and Winnie Bright, my parents.

They were tough people, hard workers, and not necessarily opposed to their oldest son going off to war. But they were also not above sending the law after him if he ran away to do it against their wishes. When I didn't come home from school that day and they figured out that I didn't go to school at all, they knew exactly where I was going.

Ever since the United States entered World War II, I'd begged them to let me enlist. Once I turned seventeen, all I needed was for them to sign a waiver allowing me to join up.

"Finish school," they insisted. "Get your education and then you can make your own decision."

I lost count of how many times I'd heard it over the course of that year. They tried to talk to me like an adult, but usually those conversations ended with me stomping out of the house. I was no adult. But I was young and patriotic and idealistic, three things that when put together are terribly difficult for parents to overcome.

When I got home from my failed journey to the recruiting station, I let my parents say what they had to say. And then I took my turn. I told them that I was sorry to worry them but my mind was made up. If they didn't let me go, I was going to run off like that again and again.

Sooner or later, I was going to make it to Pecos.

I think they saw what they were up against and knew that I meant what I said. The next morning, they relented. On October 17, 1942, I was sworn into the Navy for the duration of the war.

Along with a large group of young Texas boys, I boarded a train to the Great Lakes Training Center near Chicago for basic training. Chicago being about a thousand miles from the nearest ocean, believe me this was very basic. It lasted four weeks. We barely had time to learn how to put on our uniforms. We did a little marching, listened to a few lectures, practiced making up our bunks and then we were deemed fit to fight. The Navy was kind enough to give us seven days' leave to go see our parents before receiving our orders and shipping out to God knows where.

A friend from home, J.R. Gandy, accompanied me as we headed for the train station to spend our leave in Texas. While we waited, we spotted a serviceman coming our way. He had a lot of gold on his uniform. We stood there, trying to figure out what that meant. Was he an officer?

To be safe, J.R. and I threw him a snappy salute. He didn't seem real happy about that. He stopped and told us that he was not an officer, he was a chief and the gold on his uniform had been earned by spending most of his life in the Navy. He let us know that he was totally disgusted with us, and then went on. Talk about raw recruits.

The trip between Illinois and Texas took two days each way, leaving us with only three days at home. But we spent those three days strutting around town in our crisp new uniforms, trying, mostly in vain, to impress the hometown girls. Then we packed up again, said another goodbye to our families and got back on that train.

At Great Lakes, we were ordered to board another train, this time bound for Norfolk, Virginia, where we'd meet our troopship. We didn't know where that troopship was going to take us, but I don't remember caring much. I was not the slightest bit nervous about going to war. I don't think any of the other boys were, either. Burning patriotism, I'd call it, and these boys not only wanted to go to war but were eager to go. I was proud to be among them. Sure, there were some who signed up for the Navy to avoid getting drafted into the Army and fighting out of foxholes, but even those guys were eager.

At Norfolk, after another days-long train ride, a bus picked us up and took us to the place where our troopship waited. When I stepped out on the pier, I saw the Atlantic Ocean for the first time and it blew my mind. The largest body of water I'd ever seen was a lake.

"There just can't be that much water in this world," I thought.

It was amazing. It was a life-changing moment. My future lay out there in those waters, in the choppy waves and the beaches they lapped up against.

As a young man, the sea took me to war and it carried me home. It tested my will and my courage, and it helped me fulfill a profound sense of duty. As an older man, I could not leave it. In a sailboat built from a shell in my back yard, with three wars behind me, I spent decades chasing the distant sunset across warm, tropical waters.

Since that first glimpse of freedom from the pier in Norfolk, I have been incomplete on dry land. For nearly seventy years, the sea has been my one constant. It threatened my life again and again, and it kept me afloat when everything around me sank to the darkest depths.

I am eighty-six years old as I write these words, and almost every good thing in my life can be traced, one way or another, back to the sea.

I have given it my life. In return, it gave me these memories.

WEST TEXAS

The town of my birth is a little country place called Robert Lee, named after the great commander of the Army of the South during the Civil War. Lee spent five years in Texas as a lieutenant colonel for the U.S. Army before the war, and the story was that before Virginia called him home, he once set up camp, briefly, along the Colorado River at the spot where the town later sprung up. If you were to pass through there today, it wouldn't look much different than it did the day I was born in 1925.

We left Robert Lee when I was very young, but I spent most of my childhood around small towns not far away. My father was a cowboy and we moved from one ranch to the next, wherever work was available. My mother often served as the cook, keeping all the ranch hands well fed.

The ranches usually gave us an old rundown shack to live in somewhere on the property. I was the oldest, but before long my sister, Elgene, was born and then two brothers, Charles and Jimmy. On moving in, one of my dad's first jobs was to go to work on a storm cellar. That was always a high-priority job because, in that part of the world, tornadoes are a violent fact of life. Funnel clouds always sent us running to the cellar to wait out the storm in that muggy underground hole, in company with its permanent residents, the snakes and the spiders.

A cowboy was a jack of all trades. Dad's primary duty was tending stock, be it cattle or sheep, sometimes goats. In winter, he might put out feed for them if it was a bad year, with little grass. If they were injured, he fixed them up.

He branded calves and castrated bulls. One of the old traditions is to cook the testicles in the fire used to heat the branding irons. Mountain oysters, they call them. Whatever you might think of it, they are delicious.

He'd also ride the ranch's fence lines, checking for damage and making repairs. And he built miles and miles of fences. My father took me with him sometimes, when I was very young, ten or twelve years old. We'd work all week, sun-up to sundown, digging post holes and stringing lengths of barbed wire that seemed never to end. At night, we camped on the ground, and on the weekends, we went home to replenish our supplies and wash away five days' worth of dust and sweat.

One of my earliest memories is getting thrown off a horse when I was about four years old. I always watched for my dad at quitting time and when I saw him, I ran to meet him. He'd dismount, pick me up, drop me in the saddle and lead the horse to the barn. This particular day, when he put me in the saddle, the horse spooked and began to buck. Off I went up into air and back down again into the dirt. I landed with a thud. Not a big thud but a pretty good one by four-year-old standards.

I didn't always have the best luck with animals. When I was a bit older, my parents went into town and left me home to do my chores and milk the cow. I was furious to miss out on a trip into town. When I sat down beneath her, the old cow switched her tail and smacked me in the head. This upset me more. Then she kicked over the milk bucket.

At this point, I was ready to take it out on the cow.

I grabbed a two-by-four that was lying nearby and with every bit of strength I had, I wound up and hit her square in the head. I'm not sure what I expected to happen, but as I stood there, her eyes rolled back until all I could see were the whites. Down she went.

Convinced that I'd killed her, I racked my brain, trying to think up a somewhat believable explanation. But after a few minutes that seemed like forever, that old cow roused herself and stood up on wobbly legs. She was alive.

I said a "thank you" prayer to my maker and attempted to resume my milking, but she was not pleased with me. I didn't get another drop from her that day. When I told my dad she didn't give any milk, he couldn't understand why and I wasn't about to tell him.

I had no future as a dairy farmer, but I liked school and was pretty good at it. I pulled straight A's, at least until I got into high school and discovered girls.

On one of the ranches we lived on, Elgene and I had to ride a horse five miles in the early morning darkness to catch the school bus. My dad built a pen for the horse and we kept food and water there for it during the week. I was maybe eight years old, which would have made Elgene six. Before climbing aboard the bus, I penned up the horse, put out feed for him and pulled off the saddle. It was fifteen miles to get to school from there. Then after a full day of classes, we took the bus back, saddled the horse and rode home, arriving at the shack after sundown.

When we weren't busy with school or chores, West Texas was a wonderful place to grow up. I spent my days hunting and fishing and entertaining myself on the wide plains, doing all the things that boys do in search of adventure or mischief.

I had a great collection of Indian artifacts that I picked up while roaming the countryside – arrowheads, spear points and other various tools. On one of my excursions, I brought home three baby foxes, so new that their eyes had not yet opened. I fed them with an eyedropper and, when they grew, they made wonderful pets and followed me everywhere.

Of course, being foxes, they took to killing chickens and my dad gave me the word that he was going to have to shoot them. I gave them away to a friend.

You can find all manner of wildlife in Texas, but the two that seemed most plentiful were deer and rattlesnakes. You hunted the deer, but the rattlesnakes hunted you. At least that's the way it seemed.

If you walked outside, you were almost assured of seeing a rattler. You didn't step anywhere without looking first. If someone left a door open, they'd slither right in the house. It happened more than once, and I grew up with a terrible phobia about snakes. I hate them to this day.

My father was a great trout fisherman. Of the few times I left Texas as a child, most were spent along the trout streams of Pagosa Springs, Colorado, in the summertime. The family camped out on the streams for three or four days at a time, sleeping on the ground and cooking over a fire. No tent, just a canvas to cover the bedroll if it rained. That was real camping. You tried not to think about the rattlesnakes.

Cowboy wasn't a very profitable profession, but my father could do just about anything with his hands and if he didn't know how to do it, he could learn. From a mail-order catalog, he purchased a four-book set of "Audels Carpenters and Builders Guide." After a hard day's work on the ranch, he'd come home and study those books until the wee hours by the dim light of a kerosene lamp.

He started out repairing the houses that we lived in, and later he did small building projects on whatever ranch he was working. After a while, he got so good that he gave up cowboy life altogether and started full time as a carpenter, which paid much higher wages.
We moved from Sterling City to Fort Davis when he was hired to help build an Army air field in Marfa, the next town over. He had pulled himself up by his bootstraps and built a better life for his family.

I worked odd jobs as a teenager. By fifteen, I was working in the oil fields, which as I said figured to be my life's work. I also learned to weld and rebuild drill bits in a machine shop on the weekends.

But it was another job that sent my life sailing along a different course.

In Sterling City, I worked nights at the local movie theater. I started out selling bags of popcorn in the lobby, but when the popcorn machine shut down for the night, I filled a bag for myself with whatever was left and climbed the stairs to the projection room. When the projectionist up and quit one day, I got promoted to his job.

I'd spend night after night in that tiny room watching whatever movie was showing. In those days, Hollywood pushed out one propaganda film after another, and I took a liking to the war movies. They made life in the Navy look downright exciting.

And as it turns out, it was.

LESSONS LEARNED

In Norfolk, in early December 1942, I stepped off the pier and onto the troopship, the first time I'd been aboard anything bigger than a tiny boat. When we were underway, our destination was revealed: Panama.

What I remember most about that first ocean voyage was not the anticipation of going to war for my country. No, what I remember most is vomit. There was vomit everywhere.

It was miserable. Almost every recruit was seasick. Inexplicably, I was not. So I spent most of that journey exploring every inch of the ship and trying to avoid the awful stench. It stunk so bad in the mess hall that those few of us who weren't sick would run in, grab a couple slices of bread and some cold cuts and get out before the smell overwhelmed us. We arrived two weeks later in Panama.

I was told, along with about ten others, to board a train across to the city of Balboa on the Pacific side of the island. Looking dapper in our dress white uniforms, we found our seats on the train. It was an old coal-burner, no air conditioning.

To stave off the heat, the windows were left open. But as we chugged along, it became apparent that more soot than fresh air was coming through the windows. When we reached Balboa, our uniforms and our faces were black as night. We must have been a sight reporting to our new ship in that condition.

A chief bosun's mate lined us up and marched us into the ship's shower and laundry room. In those days, a sailor had to take care of his own laundry. The chief ordered us to dump our sea bag on deck and to scrub every item we owned, then get into the shower and scrub ourselves. That was how we spent our first day aboard, getting shipshape.

The ship was the USS Sampson. It was a beautiful destroyer that had been built a few years before the war and was being stripped of all her peacetime equipment and pretty much anything that was flammable.

But while she was being prepared for war, her sailors were given liberty in Balboa. It was my first port call in the Navy, my first chance to soak up life outside U.S. borders. I had recently received my first paycheck from the United States Navy: forty-two dollars, a full month's pay. It was time for some culture. It was time for a beer.

Three of us went to town, strolled right into the first bar we saw, climbed up on a stool and ordered a drink. Within seconds, a pretty little señorita came over and asked me to buy her a Blue Moon. We hit it off from the first drink. Before long, I began to think that I must have something that really attracts women. I was most impressed with myself. I was a real lover and never knew it.

As you might have guessed, within two hours she had relieved me of my forty-two dollars. She turned away and would not speak to me again. I left the other two guys there and headed back to the ship without a dime in my pocket, but I did take with me one of the most memorable lessons of my young life. And I'll bet you that Blue Moon was nothing more than flavored water.

By the time the yard workmen finished with the Sampson, she didn't look like the same ship. With the loss of so much weight I'm sure she was also faster, and after she was ready for sea, we received our orders. Our duty was to patrol the coast of South America in search of German submarines. The Navy had gotten word that subs were being resupplied in some of the ports along the coast.

I'd been assigned to the 1st Division, Deck Force. They maintained the forward section of the ship, and the job was not glamorous. Chipping paint, scraping paint, grinding paint, and then painting over it with a new coat of paint. After one day of that, I could see this was not the place I wanted to work. I asked for and was granted permission to work in the engine room.

It was no better. It was sweltering in the bowels of the ship. We were in the tropics with no air conditioning. I broke out with heat rash so bad that I had to walk around with my arms lifted up and legs spread apart. I began to think that maybe I'd made a big mistake joining the Navy. I wanted my mother.

Then one day I stopped and looked in the electrical shop. There sat two electricians working on equipment and drinking iced tea with cooling fans on both sides of them. In that moment, I knew that I wanted to be an electrician. I had a talk with the chief electrician's mate and the next day I got my transfer.

It changed everything. I never looked back.

PEARL HARBOR

The Sampson patrolled the waters up and down the coast of South America and we made several sonar contacts. We dropped depth charges into the waters and from time to time an oil slick would rise. We suspected that we'd taken out several German subs, but we had no sure proof of it. The poor Germans were at the bottom of the ocean.

My Navy adventure, to this point, didn't much resemble the dramatic war movies I'd watched from the projection room in Sterling City. In fact, it felt an awful lot like peacetime. In between patrols, we made port stops all over South America – places like Ecuador, Chile, Peru – and I soaked up the Spanish culture. Something about the Spanish places spoke to me, and I have always been drawn to them.

I became preoccupied with visions of blue water and travel and exotic, foreign places. If it weren't for that pesky little war, what a life it would be. Sailing, exploring, new countries, new people, new adventures? I could live like this.

During the early months of 1943, the Sampson made several trips to the Western Pacific. We'd pick up a convoy in Panama and escort the ships out to the islands where the real war was being fought. We made liberty stops in such places as Bora Bora in the Society Islands of

French Polynesia and New Caledonia, but they didn't compare with the ports of South America.

In May, we picked up a convoy in Panama and headed west again, dropping them off in New Caledonia and sailing the next day for Bora Bora, returning with more troopships. Two days later, we set off for Pago Pago, the capital of American Samoa, where we picked up our sister ship, the USS Warrington, and proceeded to Pearl Harbor.

It was a strange, unexplainable feeling to be in this place where it all started. The reminders were everywhere, of December 7, 1941, the day the Japanese bombers arrived, the day that changed my life. Many of the damaged ships had been repaired and dispatched out to fight the war. But a few ships, such as the USS Arizona, could not be salvaged and were a stark reminder of why we were there.

The Japanese made a significant oversight that day. They were successful in killing more than 2,400 Americans and inflicting major damage to the Pacific fleet, but they failed to strike the dry docks and repair yards. And Americans were busying themselves there around the clock, working toward the day of victory over Japan.

The town itself was a sight to behold. Servicemen from all over the world crowded the streets. Thousands of them. They were everywhere, especially Waikiki Beach. For a dollar, you could get your picture taken with a hula girl in a grass skirt with the ocean in the background. They were doing a brisk business.

Honolulu was famous for its salad bars. They had the most gorgeous fruits and vegetables, and you could eat all you wanted for a dollar. More than once, we skipped the ship's mess at noon and ventured into town to find a salad bar.

The most thriving places were the joints with cold beer and hot girls. They were always busy. And there was also a seedy side. I guess the thing that struck me most was the whorehouse.

As we understood it then, the military, perhaps unofficially, regulated or at least permitted the operations. There was a waiting line to get in that went around the block. The girls were inspected to control the health of the thousands of servicemen who were their customers. The place became famous throughout the fleet.

From there, we picked up four troopships and a bit of good news: We were bound for Australia.

This made for a happy crew. We had heard stories about Australia, primarily that most of the country's men were away at war and most of the country's women were awful lonely. When we left Pearl Harbor, there was a ten-to-one ratio of women to men there. As we got closer, that ratio became twenty-to-one and it grew and grew. We could not wait to arrive.

We pulled into port in Sydney on August 8 but were told that there would be no liberty allowed in Australia. We set sail the next morning for New Caledonia with the saddest bunch of sailors you ever saw.

The stories about Australia – and Australian women – had been circulating through the ship for days. To be denied even a single night on the town? Well, that was more than we could stand. We went back to running submarine patrols and running convoys with little to raise our spirits.

DIVERSIONS

Without the liberty stops for distraction, life aboard a ship can get downright tedious. During the long months when we patrolled in search of submarines, one day bled into the next and on and on until you didn't knew what day it was at all. Occasionally, though, something happened to break the monotony.

Like the time I performed an emergency appendectomy. OK, that's not quite true. Here's what happened: During one of our endless patrols, one of the crew members became painfully ill and checked into the sick bay to see if he could get a little relief. Most destroyers don't carry a doctor in their crew, only a hospital corpsman. Ours was no different.

The corpsman examined the man and diagnosed appendicitis. He apprised the captain of the man's condition and recommended an appendectomy. There were two ways to go about it. Either the patient goes to the doctor or the doctor comes to the patient. But it would have been almost impossible to move the man in his condition, which left the latter course of action.

After locating a ship that carried a doctor, we pulled alongside and the doctor came aboard by what is called a high-line transfer. A steel cable is sent over to the other ship and a chair is rigged so that it can be pulled along the cable from one ship to the other. Once this was completed and the doctor was aboard, we returned to our patrol and the other ship went on its way. The doctor examined the patient and declared that the appendectomy should be done as soon as possible.

As an interior communications electrician, I was responsible for the telephone systems aboard the ship, so I rigged a direct line between the bridge and the sick bay. I was told that I'd have to stick around and man the phone in the sick bay to assist in the operation. Once everything was ready, I took a position across the operating table from the doctor. And then we waited.

Whenever we were coming into an area of smooth water, the bridge called to inform me and I let the doctor know that it would be a good time to start operating. When a rough area approached, I alerted the doctor so that he could stop and wait out the turbulent seas.

I watched as the doctor and the corpsman went to work, opening up the patient, going in and removing the appendix, and then putting him back together again. It was fascinating.

After the surgery, the doctor remained aboard until we reached the next port. The patient was up and about in a few days and returned to his regular duties. With the doctor gone, I told the corpsman that the next time a sailor came down with appendicitis, I could handle the operation.

I'd been paying attention.

On one occasion, we'd patrolled for more than three months without being resupplied. Our food was depleted and for a week the only edible thing on the ship was rice.

Rice for breakfast. Rice for lunch. Rice for dinner.

Want some dessert? Rice.

Finally, thankfully, we met up with a supply ship and transferred supplies over by high line. At the sight of fresh food, the crew went wild. I managed to get my hands on a loaf of fresh baked bread, still warm, and a block of butter. I dug out the center of the bread and placed the butter inside to melt. I savored each bite and made it last. I did nothing else all day. It remains one of the best meals I ever had.

Gambling was the biggest pastime aboard ship. It didn't matter what kind. Shooting dice was very popular, and card games. There was also anchor pool. Sailors offered up cash and took bets on the precise minute that the ship would drop anchor or throw a line over to the dock.

My story begins with the rolling dice and ends with one high-stakes hand of cards. As I lay in my bunk one day, several sailors gathered beneath me for a game of craps. I had a pad and pencil and for hours I kept track of what numbers were coming up most often. Then I hopped down, threw in my money and began betting on the numbers I'd identified during my hours of research. I lost every time. I tried other systems, too, and never got ahead.

Then one day, I tried a new game: Blackjack. Early one morning in the mess deck, I started winning almost on the first hand. I could not lose. We broke for lunch, then resumed the game and continued it all afternoon. By dinnertime, I was up more than $300.

After dinner, the game picked up again and by midnight only two players remained, me and an old chief.

He looked at my pile.

"How much do you have there," he asked.

I had $550.

"OK," he said. "I will play you one hand for $550."

"Deal the cards," I told him.

He did, and I lost.

A dozen shipmates had gathered to watch the drama play out, but when the last cards were flipped, nothing but silence. They were kind enough not to add to my misery.

In a daze, I stood and left the mess deck and walked back to the fantail. We were rolling along at about fifteen knots and I was thinking about having lost a full year's pay on one hand of blackjack.

I looked at the bright luminescent wake stretching out behind the ship and thought that anyone that dumb should step off into that wake and disappear from the face of the Earth. But it only lasted a few minutes and then I returned to reality and went below to my bunk.

I haven't gambled much since.

SYDNEY

Nearly two months after our big disappointment in Australia, we finally got something to be excited about. On the night of October 2, as we were escorting ships from Noumea, New Caledonia, to Espiritu Santo, we came upon a Japanese submarine sitting right on the surface, a rare treat for a ship like the Sampson. In fact, it was the only time the Sampson came upon a surfaced submarine during my time aboard.

Enemy subs were common, but we picked them out with sonar because they were always submerged and it got to where we didn't bother going to battle stations when the ship destroyed those subs. Only the men who handled the depth charges had to report for duty. The rest of us went about our business. I got pretty good at sleeping through a depth-charge attack, which wasn't easy because it made an awful racket.

But for the surfaced sub, we all manned battle stations and the Sampson opened up its guns on the Japanese. The sub went under and we closed in and dropped depth charges. A massive oil slick rose to the surface.

It was my first close contact with the enemy, but I don't remember being nervous or scared. It was exciting, a welcome break from the do-nothing days of patrolling or escorting convoys. To that point, the most upsetting experience of my Navy life was the Balboa bar girl who drank my paycheck – and maybe all the Australian girls who never got the chance.

Then things got interesting.

In January 1944, we were patrolling off the Solomon Islands when we ran into a storm of the highest magnitude. Waves rose between thirty and fifty feet high. The engines were set for seven knots and yet we were pushed backward.

One wave after another lifted the ship into the air until the Sampson was straddling the peak of the wave, its bow hanging over one side and its stern over the other. The prop lifted out of the water with each crest and the noise of it running in the open air was terrifying. The entire ship was going to fly apart.

When a wave fell, we plunged into the trough and the bow dove deep into the water. One wave knocked out a window, flooding the bridge.

The storm lasted the better part of three days, and I spent most of that time hunkered down in a tight spot, hanging on with both hands, a life vest never far away. The possibility was very real that the ship might sink. In all of my seagoing days, before or since, I never encountered a more vicious storm.

When at last the winds subsided and we were able to move around, we discovered that the Sampson had sustained much damage. The deck had been pushed down and the vertical beams below that braced it were bent and bowed. The life rafts and boats secured topside were all gone, lost over the side with, among other things, all our depth charges. There was nothing left.

We limped into Wilmington, New Zealand, but were told that to get the necessary repairs, we'd have to continue on to Sydney, Australia. This was what you'd call a silver lining.

We arrived on January 17 and the ship was put in dry dock until further notice. That gave us plenty of time to explore Sydney. It was like we had died and gone to heaven.

Everything we'd heard about the place was true. I didn't do the math, but the women-to-men ratio was, indeed, off the charts. All the men were gone fighting the war and the women were hungry for entertainment. You could stand on the corner and pick any girl you wanted. They'd walk right up to you and start a conversation.

Ah, Sydney. I fell madly in love with Sydney. Actually, her name was Marie Weston and she was the most beautiful thing I had ever seen. The best part of it was that she lived with only her mother, who was stone deaf. We had to write notes to her to communicate. Once she went to bed and fell into a deep sleep, the house was ours.

We came and went as we pleased and never had to worry about waking the mother. I was sure that Marie was the woman I would marry and spend the rest of my life with. I would even take the mother with the deal. There was no sacrifice too great.

One night we spent pub crawling until the wee hours, not making it home until 4 a.m. Of course, I was late getting back to the ship and when I stepped aboard I was instructed to report to the executive officer. As I stood at attention, he looked me dead in the eye.

"Bright, what do you think I should do to you for this offense?"

I didn't blink.

"Anything but restriction, sir."

He tried to keep a stern face, but he broke up laughing. He gave me some extra duty and told me I could go ashore as soon as I finished scrubbing the smokestack. Needless to say, I got right to work. After a hard day taking care of my regular duties and scrubbing that old smokestack clean, I was headed into town again.

After leaving Sydney on February 1, I corresponded often with Marie but as time went by the letters became less frequent and after a while, no more letters.

KAMIKAZE

We went sadly back to our patrols. We sailed around the Solomon Islands for weeks and were joined by a cruiser task unit and two escort carriers. Then we joined up with a task force that included four battleships.

Finally, a little action.

While the Sampson and three other destroyers guarded the carriers, they launched an airstrike on Kavieng, New Ireland, which had been taken by the Japanese in early 1942. Thousands of rounds of munitions were leveled on the Japanese at Kavieng, allowing nearly 4,000 Marines to make an unopposed landing to occupy Emirau Island, creating a base from which the north coast of New Ireland could be kept under surveillance.

The next month or so we shuttled troops to Guadalcanal, where the fighting was fierce. Then we joined up with the Seventh Fleet and became the flagship for Rear Admiral W.M. Fletcher, commander of Task Force 77. At Hollandia Bay, New Guinea, we picked up Major General Horace H. Fuller, commander of the Army elements that would go onto Biak Island, a patch of land crawling with Japanese troops.

At daybreak on May 27, the fleet began bombarding the island.

Three cruisers sent shells into the enemy airfield west of the beachhead and the destroyers pounded away at targets near the landing area. The soldiers climbed onto the beach with American ordnance exploding all around them and Japanese troops firing on them from the shore. It made me glad I was not in the Army.

In spite of all that, the landing was a success and everything was going as planned. But it didn't stay that way.

As an electrician's mate, my battle station was the mid-ship repair party on deck, so I had an unobstructed view of what happened that afternoon. With the success of the morning landing, the rest of the day had been almost relaxing until four Japanese bombers materialized above us.

The ships offshore opened up on them with everything they had, taking out the first bomber and sending it crashing into the sea. Two other bombers nearly met the same fate, but set aflame by the American guns, managed to turn and flee the area.

The last pilot must have sensed that he had few options, and when his bomber was hit, he turned it into a kamikaze missile, diving straight for the Sampson. With my mouth wide open, I stood on the deck, frozen as I watched the bomber diving at me.

This is how it ends, I thought.

Every gun on the ship blasted away and as I said a final prayer, one of the shells ripped the bomber's wing clean off. The plane rolled hard and passed between the Sampson's bridge and the smokestack.

It missed us.

My heart was beating at a rate I never imagined possible but, by God, it was still beating.

The Japanese plane crashed down onto a small ship floating beside us, a sub chaser, engulfing it in flames. We could only stand on deck and watch it burn, a miserable, helpless feeling. I never found out how many casualties they had. It must have been quite a few.

MONEY, LUCK AND LOVE

After the excitement at Biak Island, things calmed down. Our admiral and our general departed the ship. We got back under way, making stops in Samoa and Bora Bora before pulling into Honolulu. It was on this picturesque island that we got some big news: We were going back to the United States. I'd last seen American soil in December 1942, more than eighteen months earlier. We were going home.

We had liberty in Honolulu and tried our best to hit every bar on the island. I never wanted the night to end. But at midnight, the shore patrol showed up to escort the sailors out of the bars. They loaded us into paddy wagons and took us to a holding pen on the base. When they had everyone, they took us back to the ship in one drunken crowd.

On July 4, 1944, we arrived in New York at the Brooklyn Navy Yard, and that was one happy Independence Day. We were given five days' leave, not enough time to make it back to Texas to see my family but plenty of time to go a little crazy in New York.

For the better part of two years, the Sampson's sailors had been saving our money and on that day we had more cash than we'd seen in our lives – even me, even after my gambling losses. I walked off the ship with two buddies, our pockets overflowing. There was J.R. Gandy, my old friend from basic training, and Jim Bob Harris, another Texan, in case the name didn't give it away.

We checked into the Richard Arms in Brooklyn, not a large hotel but what it lacked in size it made up in cost. I can't remember how much we spent there, but it was a bundle. And worth it. For five days, we lived like drunken sailors – which, of course, we were.

When the ship was ready for sea again, we shifted down to Hampton Roads, Virginia, where we joined a convoy and headed for Europe. We were once again looking for German subs.

In the ensuing months, the Sampson made trip after trip escorting convoys across the Atlantic and back, seeing many of the war-torn ports of Europe. We visited Oran and Algiers in Algeria, Tunis in Tunisia, and Palermo, Sicily. Most of the time we would have a convoy waiting for us to pick up and head west but in two of these places we got to hang around for a few days.

In Palermo, we tied up to the dock for four days, waiting for our convoy to form up. Liberty wasn't all that great, bars mostly, and we had to be back to the ship at midnight.

One afternoon, we were sitting around wondering what to do that night when someone suggested going ashore and finding a good restaurant for some real Italian food. A few of us got into the liberty uniform and headed for town.

We found a taxi but the driver could only speak a few English words and we spoke not a bit of Italian. We tried to tell him that we wanted him to take us to a good Italian restaurant.

"Oh, yes, I know good Italian restaurant," he said.

"Can we get good spaghetti?" one of our crew asked.

"Oh, yes, good spaghetti," our driver insisted, and after a while he pulled the car to a stop in front of an impressive building.

"Is this the restaurant?" our guy asked.

"Oh, si, good restaurant. Good spaghetti," the driver said.

We stepped out of the cab and into the restaurant, which as it turns out was not a restaurant at all. What it was, was a bar full of girls. We decided that we could get dinner later.

In Tunis, the first thing I noticed was that everyone seemed to have money and lots of it. I smoked at that time and a kid came along and offered me five dollars for my pack of cigarettes. He said he would give me twenty dollars for a carton.

We could buy a carton of cigarettes in the ship's store for fifty cents. J.R. and I decided to go into business. We told the kid to bring lots of money to the ship that night, and we returned aboard and spent all our money buying cigarettes.

When night fell, we rigged a bosun's chair over the side of the bow where it was quiet and peaceful. J.R. climbed in the chair, and we lowered it from the deck, where I stood with the cigarettes, to the dock, where the boy waited with cash. I'd hand J.R. a carton and he'd pass me up a twenty-dollar bill. Again and again, until the kid ran out of money.

But then he told us he had a friend who wanted to buy mattress covers and we set the price at twenty dollars each and instructed him to come back with more cash. The covers became a ready-made suit. Some quick modifications and you had yourself a well-dressed Arab. The ship was only there for a few days and when it departed there was hardly a cigarette or a mattress cover to be found. But we had a pocket full of money when we returned to the States.

Our next overhaul was in the Boston Navy Yard and they found unexpected problems in one of the main engines, causing our time there to be extended. We could not have known then how fortunate this would turn out to be for us, and how unfortunate it was for our sister ship.

The convoy that we were scheduled to pick up could not wait, so the job was passed along to the USS Warrington, which had returned with us from the Pacific. The Warrington departed Norfolk in early September and began heading south, into the eye of what would come to be known as the Great Atlantic Hurricane of 1944.

On September 13, 450 miles off the east coast of Florida, the Category 4 hurricane, its winds in excess of 150 knots, became more than the Warrington could stand.

It sank to the bottom of the Atlantic, taking with it 248 of the ship's 321 crew members. Five officers and 68 sailors were rescued.

Some of the survivors later visited the Sampson and gave us the details of the sinking. Water coming in through a defective ventilation system flooded the engine room, knocking out power and leaving the ship helpless with no pumps and no lights. It was a miracle any of them were saved.

Also lost were the minesweeper YMS-409, Coast Guard cutters Jackson and Bedloe, plus the lightship Vineyard Sound. In all, 390 men died that night.

For the crew of the Sampson, it had been another lucky day.

Helen Ferrendini was beautiful and fiery, a dangerous mix. A mutual acquaintance in Boston introduced us and we fell instantly, madly in love, or maybe we were just mad. I proposed to her within a week and she accepted.

There was no time for an engagement ring, but we did track down a pair of wedding bands and lined up a hasty church wedding. Well, sort of. Since she was Catholic and I was Protestant, we had to be married in the church rectory.

Her parents had come to the United States from Italy in their youth and they'd passed down to their daughter the hot-blooded Italian temperament. She could go from extreme highs to extreme lows in a blink, I'd learn, but right then we were both on a blissful high.

She accompanied me when I transferred to Norfolk after the wedding to attend Gyro Compass Tech School. The gyro compass is the main compass on a ship and, before GPS came along, it was the heart of the ship's weapons and navigation systems. I had ended up as the gyro electrician on the Sampson and that had been my primary job for a good deal of time in the Pacific.

But after a week or so at the school, I became so lonesome for life on the ship that I thought I was going to die. I had been on the Sampson so long that it had become my home. Anywhere else, I was miserable.

Helen wasn't any happier. She'd gotten a job working the counter at a dry cleaner but before long she packed up and went home to her mother.

At that point, I decided, what the heck, I'll flunk a couple exams and they'll send me back to my ship. An exam was given each Friday, and when the next one came, I gave wrong answers to many of the questions. The following Monday, I was called in to see the officer in charge of the school. He sat at his desk with my test paper in front of him, a failing grade marked on it.

"I know what you are trying to pull off," he said.

He looked down and crossed out the failing grade, replacing it with a passing grade.

"Next Friday," he said, "if you turn in a failing grade, I'm going to recommend you for a court-martial."

So I settled down and finished school. During my last week, the Japanese surrendered and Norfolk went wild. I think that I kissed every girl in town that night.

What a day that was, and it was the same all over America.

MARRIAGE

I'd been in the Navy for close to three years by the time the war ended and that meant that I could be discharged whenever I wanted. I loved the Navy, but I also had a wife and I had to give it an honest shot, try to build a life in Boston and make her happy.

I requested my discharge and, with typical Navy efficiency, I received orders to proceed to San Francisco for my formal separation. The Navy then paid mileage to drive back across the country to Boston where my future awaited. Or so I thought.

I should have known Boston wasn't going to work. I'd grown up in Texas and spent my Navy years sailing from one tropical climate to the next. I have never been able to tolerate cold and snow and everything that goes with the winter – and often the fall and spring – that far north.

Boston winter settled in right about the time I did, and I had to adapt fast. I first had to find a job, and I searched day and night for anything. The good jobs were all taken by union workers. You couldn't join the union unless you were recommended by a blood relative.

With a little help from the GI Bill, I landed a job at Compton Auto Body. The government paid for a set of tools and then supplemented my pay so that I made fifty dollars a week.

Believe it or not, in 1945 you could live on that salary. But it wasn't much of a life.

We rented a place in South Boston, on a street that could only be described as the heart of the ghetto, but convenient because it was about half a mile from the body shop.

Our second-floor apartment, like the rest of the building, teemed with rats the size of small dogs. The first thing I did was buy several large rat traps. Each morning before work, I discarded the corpses and reset the snares. The next morning, without fail, the traps were full again.

Weeks passed before I woke up to empty traps, but I bested them. I had the same battle with the cockroaches and after a month or so the place was habitable.

After plenty of overtime at the shop and a side job detailing cars for rich people all weekend, I saved enough money for my own car. I found an old second-hand Plymouth with four brand new tires. With the war barely over, tires were hard to find, so I was most happy with my purchase.

Three days after buying the car, I walked out of our building and there sat my Plymouth on top of four five-gallon paint cans. My new tires were gone and the wheels, too. A policeman explained that the only way he could help me was if I had copied the serial numbers. Of course, I had not.

The officer guessed that the same guy I bought the car from took the new tires right back and put them on another car for sale. It was weeks before I saved enough for a set of wheels and used tires from a junkyard. Needless to say, I lost money when I sold the car.

One weekend, a brand new Chrysler rolled into the small garage I'd rented for my detailing operation. I promised to have it shining, and I worked all day, scrubbing and washing and waxing. When I finished, I backed the car out of the garage and ran back inside to lock the garage door. Like a fool, I left the keys in the ignition.

When I came out of the garage, that brand new Chrysler was gone.

It was that kind of neighborhood, and I was nothing more than a country boy in the big city.

By winter's end, I'd had enough. I woke up one morning and told Helen that Boston wasn't for me and I was moving back to Texas. I told her she was more than welcome to come with me. If she didn't, that was fine, too, but our marriage would be over. She thought a bit about that ultimatum and agreed to come along.

In the spring of 1946, we loaded up and headed for Texas. Her family objected but she came anyway, though she wasn't any happier about moving to Texas than I was about moving to Boston.

The war had been very profitable for my family in Texas. My father, still new to the carpentry trade when I left for basic training, thrived because the demands of war meant plenty of construction work to be done for the military. By the time the Japanese surrendered, he was a supervisor carpenter.

This was in a little town in West Texas called Pyote. It had never been much of a place. At the beginning of the war, it had wooden sidewalks, the kind you'd see in old-time western movies. It had a sheriff by the name of Tom Bowen, who wore a big hat and boots, packed a pearl-handled six-shooter on his hip and owned the only bar in town. It was one of the last real wild-west towns.

Then the Army moved in and built a huge B-29 air base. They nicknamed the place Rattlesnake Bomber Base and it was one of largest training stations in the U.S. My dad was among the first carpenters to work there.

After the war, he started buying the surplus barracks for next to nothing. He had a large rig built so that he could jack up an entire barracks, put wheels under it and tow it off the base to vacant land he owned. He'd cut each barracks in half and transform what was left into two beautiful two-bedroom houses.

The fighting men were coming home and looking for cheap housing. My dad had just what they needed and would deliver the new house anywhere the new owner wanted it. I never did know how many houses he sold, but when he was finished there weren't many barracks left on the base.

Dad also kept several rental houses in town and when I returned to Texas, he put us up in one rent free and then he helped me set up my own business, a gas station with a repair shop in the back. Our house was walking distance from the gas station, but then anything in that town was within walking distance.

The station was located on Route 80, the main highway crossing Texas at that time. Two pumps, regular and high test, stood out front. Inside the building were an office and an area for displaying car accessory items for sale. The work area in the back was about ninety square feet and stocked with every tool I'd need for repairs and body work.

My time in Boston had given me the talent to do a decent job with body work and painting. But still it seemed like every time I made a hundred dollars, the next load of gas cost me two hundred. To survive, I had to get creative.

Pyote sits in the middle of the desert and when the temperature exceeds 100 degrees, any vehicle is going to run hot. If a car pulled in with out-of-state tags, the first thing I did was yank off the radiator cap, holler and jump back from the steam that I knew would be there. I'd tell the driver he'd better do something about his hot radiator and that I had some very good radiator flush for two dollars per can. I'm ashamed to admit what I was paying for it, but let's just say it was less than two dollars.

I would drain the radiator and pour in the flush, run the car for a minute and then refill the radiator with water. And another satisfied customer drove away.

Despite my deception, I was still not seeing much of a profit, and it was more of a problem because after the war our little family was growing fast. Three sons were born in close succession. Richard was the oldest, and then came David and Kenneth.

We needed money, so I took a second job, working nights in the local movie theater in Monahans, thirty miles down the road. I worked as a projectionist, the same job I had as a teenager. Still not enough and we had to try a new approach.

Helen, growing unhappier by the day in Texas, tended the station and I took welding jobs away from the shop. I'd weld casings for water wells and built more cattle guards than I care to count. Instead of using gates in the miles of fences around the ranch land, most ranchers opt for a cattle guard. It's not a fun job to build them.

First, you dig a pit about three-feet deep – that part was killing me – then you weld sections of pipe to place over the top of the pit. The animals are afraid to try to cross it. If you want to know real punishment, try digging with a pick and shovel and welding all day when it's 105 degrees in the shade. Only there is no shade.

I often found myself dreaming of days on the Sampson, steaming along with a cool tropical breeze blowing and never a single worry about where my next meal was coming from. I longed for the sea and adventure and, of course, port visits to yet-unexplored exotic places.

And then I'd go home, sweaty and filthy at the end of a long day, greeted by a torrent of verbal abuse. It was beginning to get me down. I mean, really get me down.

After a while, all of my frustrations became too much and one evening they boiled over. After yet another exhausting day, I came home and found no dinner on the table, nor did I see any preparations for a meal at all. We hadn't been speaking to each other for two or three days, but I broke the silence.

"This is what I plan to do," I told her. "When I get up in the morning, if my breakfast is not on the table, I'm leaving for the Navy."

I awoke at sunrise to find Helen sleeping. I nudged her, and asked if I could expect any breakfast.

"No," she said, not bothering to open her eyes.

With that, I got up, got dressed, packed a small bag and went straight to a recruiting office, where I signed up for six more years in the Navy. It was January 9, 1948.

After a few months, Helen and the boys came out to San Diego. She was ready to kiss and make up. Like a fool I agreed, and we had lived together for another uncomfortable stretch before I filed for divorce.

I thought maybe she was having problems adjusting to life in Texas, and things would turn around in San Diego. But our marriage was just as bad in California. She was a miserable person to be around. I think it was her nature, that she enjoyed being miserable and feeling sorry for herself.

She never did go back to Boston. She lived out her life in San Diego, and I was told that she died not long after the turn of the century.

The divorce, the whole ugly situation put a terrible strain on my relationships with my sons. They lived with their mother for the most part, and I never grew very close with them. After a while, we lost touch altogether.

Richard, the oldest, enlisted in the Marine Corps as a teenager and they shipped him off to Vietnam. Trudging through the jungles, he contracted encephalitis and within a few days he was dead. He was nineteen.

After a military funeral, he was buried in the Fort Rosecrans National Cemetery in Point Loma, overlooking San Diego. His name is one of nearly 60,000 on the wall in Washington, and I stop and visit whenever I can.

His younger brothers both led hard and troubled lives, and I'm sure I carry most of the blame. Kenneth died in 2012. David still lives in San Diego. I have not spoken to him in fifty years.

SHANGHAI

In San Diego at the Naval Amphibious Base, I was awaiting orders when a chief came and spoke about joining the Underwater Demolition Teams. I'd always been advised not to volunteer for anything in the military, but this seemed too good to pass up.

UDT had its beginning in Fort Pierce, Florida, during the last war. The Navy knew that the Germans had constructed obstacles on the beaches of Normandy to prevent the landing of Allied troops. Someone had to clear the beach for the invasion and it was going to take experts. The first guys were called Navy Combat Demolitions Units. They were to go ashore ahead of the invading forces and do whatever it took to remove any obstacles that might block the Allies' path, leave them bunched up at the shoreline and in the water, helpless targets for German sharpshooters.

The demolition units didn't swim in those days, but rather worked from small boats. They waded ashore to get to their targets and place their explosives. More than fifty percent of the NCDU troops were casualties at Omaha Beach. After Normandy, the name was changed to Underwater Demolition Teams.

Most of the islands in the Pacific are ringed by coral reefs and, in order to land troops, the teams went in first, blew a path through the reefs and marked the channels they had made. On more than one island, the Marines came ashore and discovered a sign on the beach:

Welcome, U.S. Marines
USO three blocks to the left.
Signed, UDT

The teams also snuck onto an island before an invasion, usually at night, to recon the beach, take depth soundings and check for potential obstacles. They constructed charts of the landing area to be used for planning the invasion.

When the Japanese surrendered, UDT-21 was the first Navy unit to go ashore. Its main purpose was to demilitarize all of the dock areas, checking for mines and booby traps. Its members also collected the Japanese weapons and made sure gun emplacements were rendered safe before the ships entered port.

They were known at that time as "frogmen" and were the predecessors to today's Navy SEALs. How could an outfit like UDT not appeal to any young, red-blooded American male? I raised my hand and told the chief I wanted in.

I was taken to a beautiful beach on Coronado Strand, where I passed a swimming test, a timed run and an interview. I'd qualified and I was instructed to submit a formal request for UDT duty. I did and my request disappeared into the Navy's vast paper mill.

A few days later, my orders came through for duty aboard the USS Chilton, a troop transport. I had been hoping for another destroyer. Months later, toward the end of the year, we sailed for Shanghai, China.

The communist army was closing in on the city and the Chilton was to evacuate U.S. Marines and any Americans who wanted to leave. That was right up my alley. It sounded a bit more exciting than building cattle guards in the Texas heat.

We reached Shanghai on December 10. It was a strange operation from the beginning. We anchored in the Wang Po River, outside downtown Shanghai. Liberty was granted the following day. We could go ashore, as long as we were back by midnight.

The people were ragged and hungry and begging for money, but opium dens did strong business. As I walked along, I peeked through open doors to see foggy-eyed men smoking pipes in their bunks. They seemed the only ones left with any money at all.

When the communists moved in, that didn't last.

Gunshots pierced the air each morning as the firing squads went about their bloody work. They didn't bother to bury the dead. They heaved them into the river and we saw the bodies floating along one after another.

The drug problem was solved in a few days, and anyone who was known to have aided the soldiers of Chiang Kai-shek, enemies of the communists, died just as violently.

We had no authority to intervene, and the communists knew it. We walked the streets in full uniform and at no time did the soldiers show any aggression toward us. We more or less ignored each other.

The Chilton's mission was strictly to evacuate Americans. After taking our people aboard, we were told the big Navy base there was going to be destroyed and that we had the rest of the day to load up with anything we needed – tools, electrical instruments, that sort of thing. We took everything that we could drag back to the ship and wanted to go back for more but there was no time.

With a little help from gallon after gallon of gasoline, the U.S. military burned its own base to the ground to keep it out of the hands of the communists. Cars and trucks went up in flames, along with heavy construction equipment and all the buildings and whatever was left in them.

The communists had guns directed at the Chilton from all directions, but they never fired on us. Our allies weren't so lucky. Two British navy destroyers, the HMS Black Swan and HMS London, were a few miles up the Yangtse River when one ran aground. The other was attempting to free it when the communists attacked, killing several sailors and wounding several others.

When the Brits arrived in Shanghai, the Chilton sent over a medical team and a squad of Marines. We got underway after that but it remained tense until we broke into open water. Clear of danger, we stopped and conducted an impressive burial at sea for the British sailors.

After the service was over, the British went their own way, and we headed north to the port of Tingtao, a city not yet set upon by the communists. It was a great place and we spent the better part of two weeks exploring it. We gambled at the local race track and visited some of the other notable sites.

I started hanging out at an American joint called Mike's Little Navy Bar. After working over some of their electrical problems, I had all the free beer I could drink.

Mike's had two floors, a bar downstairs and a dance hall on the second floor. One of the projects I did for Mike was installing an alarm system. When the shore patrol showed up looking for sailors, the bartender pushed a button behind the bar and lights flashed upstairs. By the time the shore patrol made it to the second floor, they'd find all the sailors in proper uniform and no hanky-panky going on. It worked like a charm.

One of Mike's barmaids was a pretty little Russian girl, whose name I'm sorry to say has slipped from my memory. She spoke excellent English, as well as Chinese. We hit it off immediately and had some great times. But it didn't last long, with the arrival of the communist army.

I was walking up the street one afternoon on the way to her house when four soldiers with fixed bayonets stood blocking my way and signaling me to turn around. I did an about face and never saw my girl again.

A few days later we were headed home.

KOREA

Back in San Diego, I was transferred to the USS Bass, a high-speed destroyer escort that was used for transporting UDTs, the frogmen that I was waiting to join. I was disappointed at, once again, missing out on a destroyer assignment, but I soon realized why the Navy put me on the USS Bass.

On August 4, 1950, war erupted on the Korean Peninsula.

That day, we loaded the members of UDT-1 and all their equipment aboard. We left within days for Korea. For the second time in less than a decade, I was going to war.

This time it would be a far different experience.

The Bass arrived two weeks later off the east coast of Korea, in what we were told was friendly territory. The team began doing beach reconnaissance, gathering information, which was one of its primary duties.

A few days in, UDT-1 set out to survey a small cove to see if it would be suitable for bringing landing ships to the beach. The team anticipated no problems and the frogmen carried no weapons when they left the boat and went ashore. On the beach, children ran and played in the sand, stopping to beg the Americans for candy or money.

When the children disappeared, one of the Americans realized that something was wrong and yelled, "Hit the water!" A moment later, a half-dozen North Koreans popped up from behind the sand dunes and started firing.

The unarmed frogmen raced for the water and paddled for their boat, which floated nearby. Most of them swam to the sea-facing side of the boat, but one in his haste tried to pull himself aboard on the land side. As his mates were pulling him in, he was shot in the back. Another frogman was still in the water when he was shot in the head.

Marines who made it ashore later discovered that North Korean soldiers had been living there for some time, holding the villagers captive.

I was ordered the next day to report to the commanding officer of UDT-1. It was a hell of a way to get a job. They assigned me a dead man's bunk and gave me a dead man's gear.

On a chilly afternoon, the frogmen laid out the bodies of their fallen mates on a cargo hatch on the fantail for transport out of the war zone. Standing there holding my new orders and looking at the fallen frogmen, I wondered if I had made the biggest mistake of my life. But it turned out to be the best duty that I would have in my thirty years working for the Navy.

There are very few similarities in the duties of an electrician and an underwater explosives expert, but when I asked my new commanding officer whether I would get any training, he almost laughed.

"Don't worry about it," he told me. "We'll put you through training when we get back to the States."

So when I began as a frogman I had no training at all. The only diving I'd done had been in a swimming pool and the only experience I had with explosives was helping my dad blow holes in rocks with dynamite when we were building ranch fences.

War first, train later.

At the beginning of our involvement, most of the American forces were far from combat ready and the South Korean military was ill-equipped. The North Koreans were advancing south and General Douglas MacArthur needed a way to slow them down. Frogmen knew explosives and knew how to use them, and so we became one of the keys to his new strategy.

I found myself dropping off high-speed boats and swimming onto strange beaches under the cover of night to destroy bridges and tunnels on the highways and train lines the communists might use to push farther into the South. This was the first time UDT had gone so far inland, something that would be far more common in future fights under the Navy SEAL designation. But in Korea, we were learning as we went.

The screw-ups make the best stories, and we had our share of stories. When you plan on blowing up something the size of a bridge or a tunnel, you have to pack a lot of explosives and you have to carry them on your back. If things go bad, it's hard to defend yourself if you're loaded down with two sixty-pound packs of TNT. We decided it would be great to have a security boat with a squad of armed troops go ahead of the boats that brought us and the explosives. Once the security troops had set up a perimeter, they would signal and we could come in and prepare to make things go boom.

We requested and received a squad of U.S. Marines. The guys we got were straight out of boot camp with not a bit of combat experience. The target of the first raid was a highway bridge near the beach. Our loaded rubber boats waited outside the surf line as the security boat landed and the green Marines began setting up the perimeter. Then things went bad.

The North Koreans opened up with three locked-in machine guns, spraying the entire area and hitting one of the explosives boats. We had been taught that the safest place to be at a time like this was in the water. I bailed out, along with the others, and we swam out to sea toward a tow boat that was waiting for us.

The Marines crawled into a dry creek bed, in the process managing to clog their weapons with sand so thoroughly that most of them were useless. With the few rifles still operational, the Marines held the North Koreans at bay.

A sergeant, who had been wounded, told the men to take off their combat boots, crawl to the water and start swimming. Most of them were more afraid of the dark water than they were of the North Koreans, so they hesitated. Two guys who were fair swimmers decided to give it a try. They crawled to the water's edge and paddled into the darkness.

Meanwhile, the frogs made it back to the ship and devised a plan to help the Marines. We sent one rubber boat with a four-man crew, led by Fred "Tiz" Morrison, the only black man in UDT at that time and already a living legend. He was known as "Super Frog."

The Marines were unbelievably lucky. With only the moon for illumination, they managed to swim into view of Tiz and his crew. The two Marines were pulled aboard and led the boat back to the dry creek bed, where the other Marines were barely holding off the enemy.

With the arrival of frogmen, the rest of the Marines hit the water and grabbed onto a line tossed from the boat. They held on as Tiz's crew towed them through the surf to the safety of the ship.

With everyone back on board and the ship getting underway, I could hear the North Koreans firing at ghosts on the beach. More likely, they were shooting at each other.

After that operation, those inexperienced U.S. Marines were replaced by a squad of commandos from the British Royal Marines. I remember two things about those guys. First, I don't recall a single one of them ever taking a shower. And second, when it came to a mission, they were as good as it gets. We'd send them ashore and within minutes, the landing area was clear. They were fast, stealthy and violent when necessary. After we teamed with them, we never had another problem.

MINES

While we spent some time ashore, reducing bridges and tunnels to rubble, the heart of UDT was always in the water. We lived for that and we were damn good at it. And the North Koreans kept us busy.

A big part of our job was neutralizing the mines that floated throughout the Korean Peninsula. The North Koreans released more floating mines than you could count. They were everywhere.

Our method of disposal was to swim over to a mine, place a pack of explosives and blow it up from a safe distance. Of course, when there were too many to deal with one by one, which was often, we'd sit in a boat and fire at them with rifles until they detonated.

We worked in open boats, wearing only our rubber exposer suits with diving underwear beneath the rubber suit. Few places on Earth are as cold as Korea in the winter. In the rain and sleet and snow, in sub-freezing temperatures, ice formed on the outside of our suits. We had to keep moving and keep breaking off the ice before it had time to thicken.

If we could get a break and pull up on the beach, we almost always had a load of C-3 or C-4 plastic explosive in the boat and we found that if we broke off a small chunk of the stuff and threw it into a fire, it

53

burned but did not explode. We'd sit around the fire, each holding a block of C-3, every so often pinching off bits and tossing them into the flames. We could maintain a good fire this way and keep warm as toast. Only problem was that if someone tossed in a piece that was a little too big, the fire roared as if you had dumped gasoline into it.

One day, a wise guy tossed an entire block into the fire. We all saw this and took off running as the flames shot a hundred feet into the sky. No one ever tried that again.

In late 1950, the Navy ordered a team of frogmen and a squadron of minesweepers to clear Wonsan Harbor of mines. Reconnaissance showed us the mines and their locations, moored below the surface of the water. Snow covered the ground and the icy water was bone chilling. We marked the mines with small surface markers, then detached them from their mooring cables, towed them out of the area and exploded them with gunfire. We cleared the entire harbor and the minesweepers had not arrived.

The next morning, we were back in the water at 5 a.m., checking to see if we had missed anything. To our astonishment, we found the harbor full of new mines. The enemy had slipped in with fishing boats and replaced them during the night. By noon, the wind was howling, creating white caps and four-foot swells that made our job much harder.

Early in the afternoon, we were recalled to the boat and we cheered when we saw the minesweepers arriving. But our enthusiasm was short-lived. The lead sweeper exploded in a geyser of spray. Then a second minesweeper exploded. Enemy shore batteries opened up on the sinking ships as we raced across the harbor to rescue the crew members.

U.S. destroyers fired on the shore batteries, silencing them. After dragging the crew members out of the water, some dead and some wounded, we slipped back into the frigid water and cleared all the mines again in our own low-tech way.

We patrolled all night with silent underwater exhaust, and caught three enemy fishing boats trying to re-mine the harbor. This time the enemy boats were sent to the bottom in blazing flashes of machine gun fire.

The following morning, our troops stormed ashore, only to find that a South Korean unit advancing on land had taken the port the day before. The operation had cost twelve lives on the two minesweepers and the frogs risked our own lives for many miserable hours in the frigid water. But I guess it was another step in the forgotten war.

As much as we tried, we could never get all the mines. There was always the fear of one more mine floating out there, waiting to explode, to kill. I remember vividly one occasion in which we had no sooner dropped our anchor than I heard a lookout screaming that a mine was floating toward us.

I looked to the water and held my breath. The mine was powerful enough to sink our ship and most any other in the fleet. It struck the bow and eased along the starboard side, feet from me, bouncing repeatedly – bump, bump, bump. Then it just floated away.

It was a dud.

RAISING THE DEAD

One of the mantras of the American military is the idea of "no man left behind." This includes the dead. Especially the dead.

If a man gives his life for his country, his fellow servicemembers will do everything in their power to recover the body and return it to American soil. The nation owes that to him. And it owes it to that man's wife or his children or his mother, to bring the fallen hero home so that they might be able to say a final goodbye. It is a good and noble concept, but it is not always easy. Death in war comes violently and unpredictably. When death came in the water, they called UDT.

The plane crashes were the worst and as the war dragged on, more and more planes went down, ending up scattered and broken at the bottom of the Yellow Sea or the Sea of Japan, or some other river or tributary. The dead were there, too, and it was our job to get them out.

We'd arrive by boat, if the crash site was nearby, or flown in if it wasn't. The work was miserable and morbid and cold. The first step was to identify the aircraft and then, whenever possible, bring the victims to the surface so they could be identified and sent home. Most often in the aftermath of crashes, we weren't so much raising bodies from the water as retrieving body parts – an arm, a leg, a torso.

As team members were diving on one crash site, one of our guys became disoriented in the dark water. He was relieved to see a hand reaching out to him and thought his dive partner was offering assistance. He grabbed the hand, but then realized it was attached only to a severed arm. Startled, he kept his grip and brought the arm to the surface. That was the job.

The arm might well have been the only piece of that servicemember that could be located, but it went home. And that man's family got a casket and a funeral and closure.

TAKAYAMA

During the war, we kept a home base at Camp McGill in Japan, and if we were able to leave Korea for a short break, this was our destination. McGill was an old World War II Japanese army base in Takayama, a small town about fifteen miles west of Yokosuka, where the U.S. Navy maintains a base today.

The area surrounding McGill, with its many saki bars and houses of ill repute, was declared off limits to us and, to be sure, it was patrolled by military police. Of course, we were not the type to let something like that stop us and it became a great game, a contest between the Underwater Demolition Teams and the military police.

We considered the off-base area our training grounds and when we weren't on duty we often found our way to the restricted part of town. We figured that if we could not evade the MPs there, we would never survive behind enemy lines in North Korea. So that's how we spent most of our liberty time, going into town in our working greens or whatever we happened to have on at the time.

Instead of leaving by the main gate, we went under, over or through the chain-link fence that surrounded the base. Then we would gather at a saki house for an evening of drinking and general hell raising, returning to the camp before sunrise.

The Marine MPs caught on to our night operations and they were determined to put a stop to them. This raised the stakes and made the game more exciting. One night, a large group gathered at one of our favorite spots. We stationed a boy outside to watch for MPs.

Many hours and many drinks later, we had few cares in the world, until the boy ran inside shouting "MP! MP!" We bolted outside like we were shot out of a gun. About a dozen team members took cover with an old Japanese truck in the parking lot. They got under it, in it, on top of it, any place there was room to squeeze in a body. The rest of us hunkered down in the weeds and bushes.

Within seconds, an MP jeep pulled up and the driver turned off its lights and killed the engine. Everything was still and quiet. Something was going to have to give, and the tension began to build. Out of the silence, I heard a rustling behind me. One of the guys leapt out and screamed: "Those bastards are hiding in the truck!"

The scene that followed was chaos – MPs yelling and men running in every direction, to say nothing of the damage inflicted on that old truck as a dozen drunken frogs tried to extricate themselves from their hiding places and escape capture. A few were caught and they spent the night in the brig, but most of us made a clean getaway and returned to camp.

After a few of these nights on the town, the beaches of North Korea seemed almost peaceful.

CEASE-FIRE

The end of World War II came suddenly and joyously and decisively. The enemy surrendered and the Allied forces had won. All of America celebrated and most of the world joined in. There was drinking and dancing, shouting in the streets. I will never forget that day.

Korea was nothing like that.

By 1952, all the politicians and military leaders were looking for a way to end the war, but the peace talks dragged on and on. It was a slow, brutal process until one day, in July 1953, an armistice agreement was signed. There were no celebrations, no ticker-tape parade down the Canyon of Heroes in New York.

Since early 1951, we'd settled into a routine in which our team, UDT-1, rotated every three months with UDT-3. We'd spend three months in Korea and then return to our home base in California for three months to decompress and train.

We'd rotated in and out of Korea so many times during the war that by the time it ended I don't remember any homecoming at all. At some point, we rotated home and never went back.

DISCIPLINE

At Coronado after the war, mornings were spent maintaining our equipment and in the afternoons we did physical training. Most days, we went for a distance swim and then laced up our combat boots for a good, long run in deep sand. Or at least what looked like a good, long run.

Del Coronado Hotel Beach wasn't far from our training area. It was always full of good-looking girls sunning themselves and every chance we got we jogged down, jumped over the jetty and sunbathed with the girls. Then we ran full-out all the way back to the base at quitting time, arriving out of breath and dripping with sweat like we had finished a five-mile run. It really impressed the troops.

Often we carried out night operations and war games by attacking the ships in San Diego Harbor. We'd make long swims using SCUBA gear and close in on the ship. They had been told that we were coming and would be on the lookout. Most of the time, we made it to the ship and set off flares, which indicated we had blown up the ship. Sometimes we were able to swim up undetected, climb aboard and take prisoners – just for fun.

On weekends, spearfishing was our thing. We organized a skin diving and spearfishing club and trained a number of local boys how to dive and fish. Most of them later joined the Navy and the best of them joined UDT.

We'd take off to Mexico for days at a time, bringing nothing but our spearguns and sleeping bags. We'd catch fish, lobster and abalone, and sleep on the beach. It was a great way to live. We participated in several international spearfishing meets and had a lot of fun but never won the big prize.

Of course, spearfishing wasn't the only reason a bunch of young, rowdy sailors ventured down into Mexico. Our outfit, as far as discipline was concerned, was what many captains and a few admirals considered "a disgrace to the United States Navy." Funny, though, they always called on us to do the tough jobs.

Being a little wild tends to go hand-in-hand with being good at the type of work the UDT guys were asked to do. For certain jobs, you've got to be a little crazy. I imagine it's much the same with today's Navy SEALs.

Standing in formation one morning as the roll was being called, the men remained silent as four names went unanswered. The officer in charge asked if anyone knew the whereabouts of these men. Someone responded that they were locked up in the Tijuana jail.

Our executive officer at the time was a hard-charging lieutenant named Wendy Weber. Wendy went on to have a great career in the Navy, rising to become a captain, but in those days he was as wild as the rest of us. He volunteered to take his jeep down to Tijuana and bring back his incarcerated sailors. Only Wendy didn't come back and the next word we got was that Wendy was locked up in Tijuana right next to the original four.

That's a leader.

In fact, he was probably the only guy who could control us. Years later, when Wendy was a captain, I reminded him of that story. He smiled and said, "Those were the days."

INDIAN HEAD

Because of the many floating and underwater mines we had to contend with in Korea, our command requested that a course be set up for us at the Explosive Ordnance Disposal School in Indian Head, Maryland.

The improvised three-month class covered mines and torpedoes and about ten of us from UDT-1 reported there in January 1952, hoping to return to Korea with an edge that would help us in our never-ending quest to render the surrounding waters safe for the troops. Like Korea, the weather in Maryland was frigid and a foot of snow covered the ground when we arrived.

The course began with some brief dive training, which was fine because we'd lived in the water in Korea. But the cold has a way of sucking the fun right out of the job. Most mornings, we had to break the ice on the Potomac River to get to the water and once we were in it, we found the floor of the river was made up of thick, soft mud that was ten-feet deep.

In one of our exercises, we hauled a high-pressure hose down to the river bottom. The job was to wash out a tunnel under the muck twenty feet long and then turn around and come back out the way we came. It was good test for claustrophobia.

At night, we cleaned up and hit all the joints in town. Indian Head is about twenty-five miles south of Washington, D.C., but the Navy base there is the last stop on a dead-end highway, bordered by the Potomac River, and if you're there, you have a reason to be there. Nobody is just passing through.

Still, at that time, it was pretty wild for a tiny dot on the map. Slot machines were legal and they were everywhere in town, even in barbershops and gas stations. It was no problem finding a place to eat and drink and have a good time.

On the base, next door to the school, was a restricted area called the Navy Power Factory, where the service developed its big guns and big explosives. Earth-shaking blasts were a part of life at the Power Factory. Nearly every day something would go off and rattle the whole town. Most of the residents paid it no mind and asked no questions, unless it happened to blow out the windows of their house, which was not uncommon.

Partying, explosions, a little diving mixed in. The place suited us fine.

But after the diving portion of the class was done, the training turned much more serious. We learned the names and composition of nearly every explosive compound on Earth. We learned how to make our own explosives out of everyday ingredients. We studied every piece of underwater ordnance in the U.S. arsenal and the arsenals of other militaries throughout the world.

One at a time, we learned to disassemble them and render them harmless. To prove how serious the job was, instructors rigged the dummy ordnance with small explosive charges so that if you made a mistake, it would go off like the real thing. It was enough to let you know you'd screwed up. In the real world, in Korea, if you screwed up, you died. Not only that, a lot of other people would die, too.

Once the second phase of training kicked in, there was no more boozing. After dinner, we went back to the classroom to go over what we'd learned that day. The entire class was there, hard at work. We'd seen enough in Korea and knew these things could kill. We'd seen them kill. So we were motivated to learn. There were no dropouts in our class and that was unusual.

When the three-month course ended, we packed up to head back to Coronado. Most of us had driven across country, and one member of the team had pulled his small camping trailer to Maryland. He told some of the guys that he had plenty of room and invited them to toss in their suitcases or extra sea bags so they would have more space in their own vehicles for the long drive home.

Back at Coronado, days later, this guy was the last to show up and he arrived without his trailer. He told the guys he was real sorry but he'd had a bit of an incident on the way home. He was driving a back road through the hills of Georgia when he turned his head and saw his trailer rolling right past his car. A runaway bullet.

The trailer left the highway, went airborne and fell 300 feet, turning upside-down during flight and bursting open like watermelon when it hit the ground. Clothes and gear flew in all directions. The driver said he couldn't figure out how to get down to the scene of the disaster, let alone attempt to retrieve all the lost items strewn about. So he kept on driving. I got a big kick out of that, mostly because none of my gear was in his trailer.

I enjoyed the EOD course, the first formal explosives training I'd received since joining UDT. I liked it so much that years later, after the war ended, I requested the full six-month course. It was 1955 when I returned to Indian Head. The town and the base hadn't changed much, but the Power Factory was renamed the Naval Propellant Plant and had begun making rocket propellant using new smokeless powder. There were fewer explosions and things were much calmer.

The first three months of the full course repeated the shorter course I'd taken. During the last three months, we were schooled on a much wider variety of explosives – bombs, artillery shells, booby traps, nuclear weapons.

We'd study them in the classroom and head out into the field where we'd have to locate them, dig them up and disarm them as you would in a war zone.

Most of the students were old hands, with years of experience in the various services. There were quite a few students from foreign countries, too. As before, the subject matter was taken very seriously and most of the students stayed up late into the night trying to keep up with the material.

EOD technicians are every bit as important in today's military as they were then, maybe more so. The wars in Iraq and Afghanistan challenged U.S. troops to always be on the lookout for what came to be known as improvised explosive devices. The crews proved their worth out there day after day, most of the time sniffing out the bombs before they could do any damage. But like in Korea, you can never get them all, and it's heartbreaking to see so many troops killed and maimed. The casualty rate for EOD techs in the modern wars is among the highest in the military.

The EOD school is now located at Eglin Air Force Base in Florida. I had the good fortune to tour the place once and some of the equipment and the new teaching methods made my head swim. I can't say enough good things about the EOD community, but a big piece of my heart will always be with the underwater demolition teams and the Navy SEALs that succeeded them.

A big piece of my heart will also always reside in Indian Head. I didn't know it when I left there for the second time in 1955, but that little Southern Maryland town would change my life forever.

KODIAK

In UDT, we never stopped looking for new and better ways to do our jobs, to carry out missions with quickness and stealth. Sometimes the new ideas worked, sometimes they didn't. Sometimes it fell somewhere in between.

In the mid-1950s, our team bought four sailing kayaks from the Germans. They were called foldboats, sixteen-foot-long vessels that could be broken down to the size of a large suitcase. They'd been equipped with a main sail and a jib, plus leeboards to keep them on course.

The foldboats were sleek, easy to handle and we thought they'd do fine. For weeks, we sailed and paddled them in San Diego Bay and in the Pacific off Point Loma and Coronado. We'd been working from a submarine, the USS Perch, which had been retrofitted for covert UDT jobs, and the kayaks were the perfect complement.

After the team had grown comfortable with the foldboats, we were tapped to participate in war games around the naval station in Kodiak, Alaska. Our job once we got there would be to sail the kayaks around the north side of Kodiak Island, sneak onto the base and, hypothetically, do violent things.

First we had to get there.

Leaving Coronado, it was my job to get the Perch loaded with the UDT gear, so when we pulled up alongside the sub, I told the guys that I'd go aboard and assess the situation. We'd be berthed in the forward torpedo room in the bow of the sub and so I took advantage of being the first UDT guy aboard and staked out a good bunk.

The problem with bunks on a submarine – the problem with most things on a submarine – is there's not a lot of room. Most bunks have barely enough space to roll over, so I eased in and threw my sea bag on a top bunk, which had plenty of space above it. I went back to the dock and told the guys where we'd be staying. I told them they could pick any rack except the one where I'd thrown my bag.

Of course, my little plan backfired. It didn't take long after we got underway for me to realize that my bunk was beneath the hydraulic drive motors and they were noisy, damn near impossible to sleep under. To add to my misery, hydraulic fluid leaked and I spent much of the trip hanging tin cans to catch it. I'd really outsmarted myself there.

The Perch traveled first to Honolulu, running along the surface all the way. It was a snorkel boat and the tip of the snorkel was all that protruded above the water line. Each time a wave rolled over, its valve closed and the air pressure inside the sub changed. After a few days, your ear drums flapped around like window shades.

We arrived in Honolulu after a little more than a week, stayed two days and then set the course for Alaska. That northern run was uneventful, except for one day about midway through when the captain decided the sub was due for a field day, which meant the crew would stop and clean the entire sub. We'd be in the way, so he ordered us to inflate one of our rubber boats and hang out on the surface until they'd finished the job.

Once we were set up in the rubber boat, the Perch submerged and disappeared, leaving us with time to kill. It didn't take long for us to get going a game of King of the Mountain. I've often wondered what a pilot flying overhead might have thought to see eight men floating in the middle of the Pacific Ocean, roughhousing and laughing.

But after a couple of hours, the sub picked us up and we were on our way again. The trip from Hawaii to Alaska took more than two weeks.

We arrived at our destination on the north side of Kodiak Island and surfaced under the cover of night. The plan was to sail four kayaks around the island and then try to infiltrate the base. We'd go ashore during the day and travel only at night. The kayaks were loaded with sleeping bags and rations, and I thought we had a fun trip ahead. The first night proceeded without incident until we started working our way toward the beach. The surf was brutal, much bigger than we'd anticipated, and it took hours to find a place we could land without getting smashed to pieces.

Daylight had sprung by the time we made it to shore and as we stepped onto the beach, we heard a helicopter approaching, surely participating in the war games. We had no time to do much of anything. We left the kayaks and all the supplies where they lay and raced into the woods.

That's where we were, hidden and silent, when we watched the helicopter land and capture all of our gear. I figured we were pretty well beat, but the lieutenant in charge of the team had other ideas.

"Hell with it," he said. "We'll walk in. It's only fifty miles."

So off we marched ever deeper into the woods. A fifty-mile hike is bad enough, and without food is even worse, but throw in the mountain that stood before us and I had to recalibrate my thinking. This was not going to be any damn fun at all.

We started to climb and climb some more. I was relieved when we reached the top of the mountain, but my relief was short-lived. The summit provided a beautiful view into the valley below and a not-so-beautiful view of another mountain that we'd have to climb.

As we walked, one of the guys, Billy Dishman, spotted a pile of manure sitting atop a boulder. Billy was fresh out of training and recently assigned to our team.

"I was raised on a farm in Kentucky, and I never seen no cow shit on top of a rock like that," he said.

I could only laugh.

"Dish, that's not cow shit," I said. "That's bear shit."

After that, Billy was a bundle of nerves. If someone stepped on a twig, he'd jump two feet off the ground.

Kodiak Island, of course, is known for one thing – bears. And there were plenty of them on our route. While we only spotted a couple from a distance, we often heard them crashing through the woods and from that point on, Billy was ready to run and hide every time one of those bears made its presence known.

We were unarmed so we had nothing to protect ourselves should one of them attack. If we had been armed, we might have hunted them for food. Instead, we subsisted on salmon berries. Each time we spotted a berry bush, we'd stop and fill our pockets. For three days and two nights, we feasted on those beautiful red berries and, to be honest, they tasted pretty good. We washed them down with water from the streams.

On the third day, we came upon an abandoned campsite. No doubt it belonged to Marines out looking for us. When they moved on, they left behind packs of sugar, chocolate and coffee from their rations. We stuffed them in our pockets and used them to flavor the salmon berries.

At the end of the third day, we arrived at the naval station, skirted the perimeter and came upon a drainage ditch, which we crawled through to access the base. From there, it was a breeze. We snuck into the main building, walked through the door of the officer in charge and informed him that we'd destroyed the base. Then we asked him where we could find some real food.

Though not according to plan, we'd accomplished our mission and had time to kill as the war games were winding down. I checked into the chief's quarters and struck up a quick friendship with one chief who was also the base's game warden. He took me along on his rounds the next day and we found time to get in some excellent salmon fishing.

Another chief, a pilot, took me out flying in his seaplane and as we floated above Kodiak, we spotted one of our crews bringing a boat into the island. The chief glanced at me with mischief in his eye and suggested we have a little fun with the fellas. As he manned the controls, I gathered a box of toilet paper from the back of the plane and strapped myself in beside the open door.

Then the pilot commenced to dive on the boat and I commenced to bombing it with roll after roll of toilet paper. It was quite possibly the first toilet-paper bombing in the history of the U.S. military. I managed a couple of direct hits and all the boys on the boat could do was look up and shake a fist at us.

JACQUES COUSTEAU

During most of our hiatuses from Korea, when we returned to California for training, our focus was on diving. One of the capabilities that the Navy was learning to utilize was SCUBA and in 1951 we were introduced to the latest diving technology by none other than Jacques Cousteau.

The world-famous French explorer visited Coronado to show us the Aqua Lung diving rig, which had been developed by the French and not yet gone on sale in the United States.

The great thing about it was that it used compressed air rather than oxygen and was self-regulating. The proper amount of air was available to the diver at any depth and it would change automatically if the diver went deeper or ascended toward the surface. This did away with a multitude of problems associated with the earliest SCUBA units and it opened up more possibilities.

Around that time, Rene's Sporting Goods in Los Angeles imported a few sets of the first units from France, specifically for the UDT teams at Coronado. To that point, we'd done some occasional SCUBA diving but only with basic oxygen-recirculating outfits. The advantage of these rigs was that they made no bubbles that might reveal your location to the enemy.

The downside? They were very dangerous.

If you exceeded a depth of thirty feet, you were tempting disaster. Any number of things could go wrong, leaving you with a splitting headache or, worse, unconscious in the middle of the dark sea. We were eager to find a diving outfit that was safe and easy to use.

The first dive we made with the Aqua Lung was an odd one. In the Pacific Ocean, off the coast of San Diego, four of us – led by our renowned skipper Douglas "Red Dog" Fane – dove down to a U.S. Navy submarine sitting on the ocean floor sixty-five feet beneath the surface.

Before the dive, I asked Fane if there was anything special I should know about the Aqua Lung unit. In his typical dry style, he pointed to the mouthpiece and told me: "Put that in your mouth and breathe."

The four of us dove down to the submarine, climb inside and have a cup of coffee with the crew. Entering and exiting a submarine is referred to in diving terms as "locking in" and "locking out." It's quite an experience, with the latter being the stranger of the two.

The escape trunk is a compartment about six-feet high and four feet in diameter, just room enough for two divers with tanks on their backs. You climb up a ladder and close the hatch behind you. You open a valve that allows the compartment to fill with seawater, which rises slowly to your waist, then to your neck and over your head until the space is full. If you have any trace of claustrophobia, it will reveal itself when you flood that escape trunk.

Once the water pressure is equal to that outside the submarine, you can open the exit hatch and swim out. There was always a feeling of overwhelming freedom as I emerged into open water.

After that successful first dive, we spent a week at Rene's Sporting Goods, learning to repair and maintain the Aqua Lung regulator. The shop stocked hundreds of spare parts and the teams were buying them up. By the time the week was through, we each had enough parts to build our own regulators.

Back at Coronado, we found surplus oxygen tanks in the scrap yard and converted them into dive tanks. We'd gone nuts over the new Aqua Lungs. We used them almost daily in our work and when the weekend rolled around, we used them for spearfishing and catching lobster.

This was all before wet suits became standard diving gear. The only exposure suits at the time were dry suits that you wore over a set of long underwear. And without fail, they leaked. We got so sick of it that many of us would skin dive all winter long, wearing only our swim trunks and maybe a sweatshirt. As you might suspect, it tested your nerve and fortitude. We called ourselves "The Badass Club."

In 1952, we got wet suits and we thought we'd died and gone to heaven. That was one giant step for the frogmen.

During the early 1950s, Cousteau dropped by every so often to see how we were progressing with the Aqua Lung. Sometimes he came along on our spearfishing outings, usually out to the Channel Islands nearest to San Diego. On one of those trips, I made quite an impression on him.

Cousteau brought along a case of French wine and between dives we stopped for a drink or two. During one sipping session, he asked us to spear as many moray eels as possible, because he loved to eat them. Before we returned home, I speared a big one, and I mean it was big. We were in two boats and as we prepared to head back, I was on one boat and Cousteau was on the other. I held up the big moray and ask him if he wanted it.

"Yes," he yelled to me.

Without hesitation, I muscled up and heaved the eel over to the other boat. My toss was on target, maybe too good, because the eel hit Cousteau right in the face and wrapped itself around his head before he could grab it. We all had a big laugh about it, including Cousteau.

And with that, I imagine, I became the only man to ever wrap an eel around the head of the famous Frenchman.

LEAD SHOES

As we got more serious about our diving, we trained on all types of SCUBA and became experts at just about everything. The only area in which we couldn't claim expertise was deep-sea diving, better known as hard hat.

When most people think of old-time SCUBA diving, the image that pops into their head is that of hard-hat divers. With the giant copper helmet, lead belt and lead shoes, you looked like an underwater astronaut. All the gear weighed more than 200 pounds and it was awful to walk around in it on land. But in the water, you didn't notice it at all and you could do things that weren't possible with other SCUBA rigs.

"Why not do it all?" I figured. So I asked to go to Deep Sea Diving School in Washington, D.C. They handed me a set of orders and away I went driving across the country.

It was 1957 and around this time I'd taken a liking to sports cars. My ride was a 1956 Austen Healey, two-toned, black with red down the sides and matching black-and-red leather interior. It was flat-out cool, and in the middle of the night out on the Arizona desert, I began to put the pedal down. A fast car and an open highway. It was a beautiful thing.

After a while I noticed headlights behind me, but thought nothing of it. I was rolling along around 90 miles per hour and thinking to myself, "Me and the guy behind me are sure putting some miles behind us." That's when the red lights came on.

The policeman noticed that I was military, and he asked to see my orders. When he saw that I was going from Underwater Demolition Teams to Deep Sea Diving School, he was intrigued.

"Did you ever see an octopus down there?" he asked.

I saw my opening. I started telling sea stories, figuring I'd make a friend and get out of a nasty speeding ticket.

Hell yes, I'd seen an octopus and if he liked that he'd like the next story and the next one. A half-hour later, we might as well have been old pals. I'd be on my way, scot-free any minute, I was certain. But as I finished up one last story, he smiled and pulled out his ticket book.

"Can't we just forget it this time?" I asked.

"I'd like to," the officer said, gesturing back toward his car, "but that guy that's with me is a real SOB."

So after almost an hour chatting this guy up on the side of the road, I pulled off with a speeding ticket in hand and a lighter foot on the gas pedal.

HAZEL

I arrived at the Deep Sea Diving School in early December 1957 and it was a bit like coming home. I'd spent nearly a year in the D.C. area between my two stints at EOD training. I'd made many friends there, so this time around I often visited Indian Head on weekends.

Not long after I was back in town, two of these friends, Eugene and Kay Sopchick, started scheming. They kept telling me about this friend of theirs named Hazel and they insisted they introduce us. I don't remember resisting too much and I certainly didn't complain after I met Hazel. I was never the same again.

I could not believe how beautiful she was, and she had a personality more wonderful than her beauty. The first thing I recognized about her – OK, the second thing – was her intelligence. She was everything you would ever want in a woman.

She liked me too, and from that first meeting, we spent every spare minute together. I worked eight hours a day, drove to see her after clocking out and made it back to Washington around 4 a.m., in time to sneak two hours of sleep, go to work and start the cycle all over again.

Hazel was a package deal. She had three young daughters. Her twins, Sandie and Andie, were twelve and Terri was five.

I fell for her girls, too.

My courtship of Hazel only intensified with time, the days flying by so fast I barely recognized the turning of the pages on the calendar. But soon enough, sure enough, my six months at diving school ended and I had to return to California. I left her with a promise that when I returned to San Diego, I'd see about pulling some strings and getting back to Maryland.

Back on the West Coast, all I could think about was Hazel and the girls. I wanted to do something to prove that to them and I racked my brain searching for the perfect gift. Then I found it. Or rather, I found him. Mike was a young Boston terrier pup. I bought a cage and shipped him by rail to Maryland. I called Hazel and told her that a surprise was on the way.

When the package arrived, Mike was an instant hit with the girls, but he needed a little training. On the first day he was left alone in the house, he yanked the telephone off its table and chewed up the receiver cord. The following day, they got smart, or thought they did, and left him in the bathroom, believing he could do no harm penned up there for the day.

When they returned, they found that he'd pulled down the shower curtain and the largest piece remaining was no bigger than a postage stamp. But with all his faults, they loved him.

For the next six months, Mike kept an eye on the girls for me as my relationship with Hazel continued with each of us on a different coast. We wrote one letter after another and spent countless hours on the phone. I'd been plenty happy for years in San Diego, with its warm weather and beaches. Since returning from Maryland, I was miserable and couldn't wait to leave.

The last time I'd fallen this hard, the last time I'd considered uprooting myself for the sake of a woman, things had ended badly. But I knew this was different. I wasn't some fresh-faced kid just off the ship, rushing into marriage.

This relationship had lasted beyond the whirlwind courtship and endured this period of separation. I had to get back to Hazel.

Most longtime Navy people have a friend in the bureaucracy who is in a position to pull strings and get things done. I had such a friend and told him that I wanted duty as an instructor at EOD school in Indian Head. He reminded me that I would have to go to Navy Instructor School first, but assured me that it was no problem and he would take care of that, too.

In short order I was assigned to instructor school, a four-week course in San Diego, and then handed a set of orders to transfer to Explosive Ordnance Disposal School. I arrived back in Maryland in mid-August 1958 with a whole new world about to open up in front of me. I knew I was in love. What I didn't know at the time was that the next thirty-seven years would be the best years of my life.

I married Hazel a few days later, on August 22 at the home of Hazel's mother, Virginia Hicks. The ceremony was held in the living room and presided over by the Rev. Dr. M.C. Brubaker, a retired Baptist minister and a close friend of the Hicks family. With a couple of "I do's," it was done. I'd not only gained a wife but also three daughters.

From the beginning, there were never any adjustment problems with the girls. The dog, Mike, didn't hurt. But I also had another ace up my sleeve.

Before the wedding, I explained to Hazel that I only had so much money. I could afford wedding bands for us, even spring for a brief honeymoon at a nearby beach, but as for the engagement ring, I offered her an option. I told her I could buy her a nice, shiny diamond or, instead, I could take the money and buy us a boat to go with a 40-horsepower Mercury outboard motor and a set of water skis that I'd brought with me. With the girls in mind, she chose the boat.

Sandie and Andie and Terri became expert skiers and learned to jump the ramps set up in the water. We spent many wonderful weekends, boating and waterskiing on the Potomac River. The only problems I ever remember having with the girls involved trying to coerce them into doing their homework at night or, later, teaching them to drive, both of which were a test of wills and not for the timid. But we got through it.

And years later, Hazel finally got her diamond ring.

Of course, Hazel didn't have to count on me for money. She was a talented contract negotiator for the federal government and always brought home a bigger paycheck than I did. Throughout our married life, it developed into a friendly competition. I always strived to surpass her, but each time I earned a promotion it seemed she'd get one a few days later. I never did get ahead of her. We laughed about it a lot, and I was man enough to take it.

In later years, after we'd both retired and were living in Florida, she got into real estate and talked me into taking the state exam. There was a required two-week training course, and I decided it would be my last chance to outdo her.

The school was in Miami and every night after class, I stayed up into the wee hours studying, surrounded by stacks of notes and books. I lived like a hermit for those two weeks, took the final exam and was thrilled to score a 96.

When I got home and presented her my grade, she stood up and walked away. I'd beaten her, I knew it. But she came back a moment later with her exam: She'd scored a 98.

SHIPWRECKS

When I reported to my new gig as an instructor at EOD school, I was assigned to teach diving, which was natural since I was coming from almost a decade with UDT. But when the bosses learned that I'd also been a chief electrician's mate, that combination of skills prompted them to switch me to a job teaching nuclear weapons disposal.

I was given a top-secret clearance and began instructing the next generation of troops how to disassemble and render safe weapons so powerful that they'd make the two nukes dropped on Japan in World War II seem no bigger than firecrackers.

I was enjoying the turn my life had taken. I had a happy home and in my spare time I took college courses and taught electronics to some of my shipmates.

My orders at EOD school had been for three years, but I didn't want to uproot my family, so I reached out to the same guy who had secured me a spot teaching at the school. I told him I needed an extension of duty. As a reward, I promised him a good bottle of Scotch whiskey.

A few days later, true to his word, he told me it was all set, and I handed over the most expensive bottle of Scotch that I could find.

It wasn't much later that I discovered all instructor positions had been frozen indefinitely. I couldn't have left if I'd wanted to. I never did get that bottle of Scotch back.

During my time at EOD school, I sometimes got tapped to take on other assignments. In the summer of 1960, my commanding officer must have thought I needed a vacation because one day he called me in and told me I'd been chosen to lead a team that would locate and dive on the wreckage of Civil War blockade runners off the coast of North Carolina. It turned out to be one of the most interesting jobs I'd ever done. A powerful hurricane had passed along the coast off of Wilmington and partially uncovered the remains of several ships.

We set up headquarters at an oceanfront hotel in Carolina Beach and the state chartered a small plane to fly us up and down the coast. Each time we spotted a wreck, we tossed down a buoy to mark the spot. Later, a few of us went back to dive those spots and determine whether what sat on the ocean floor was worthy of a more extensive salvage operation.

Meanwhile, we researched Civil War-era Navy records and in many cases we were able to determine the name of the ship and find out what it was doing and how it sunk. What a feeling it was to read about a 100-year-old ship one day and the next day be swimming among its wreckage.

Hal Waters, the pilot who flew us to spot the wrecks, was also a SCUBA diver and had been diving coastal wrecks for years. Each day, he'd ask us which wrecks looked good and which were busts. The most promising wreck was the Modern Greece, one of the last blockade runners to be sunk while attempting to reach Fort Fisher, one of the last rebel forts to fall during the war.

Naval records stated that the ship was trying to make it into Fort Fisher to unload wartime supplies during the night when the Union Navy discovered it and, with the help of shore batteries, sank the ship with gunfire.

Steam power was coming into use at that time and the Modern

Greece was a combination sail and side wheeler. Instead of a paddle wheel in back it had a paddle wheel on each side of the ship.

Its iron hull was mostly intact with the notable exception of some damage inflicted upon it by Yankees. It was sitting upright on the bottom at a depth of about forty feet.

We hit the jackpot with that ship. Enfield rifles, boxes and boxes of them, and the ammunition to go with them. Enfields were the first military rifles manufactured with a rifled barrel, which made it more accurate than the smooth-bore weapons that were common at that time. We also found a large stash of medical supplies and surgical equipment.

It wasn't easy bringing all these artifacts to the surface. We had a large air compressor, and we built an underwater vacuum with pipes and hoses. The vacuum sucked out the excess sand that remained among the wreckage and anytime the vacuum unearthed something promising, two divers would turn off the vacuum and begin removing the items so they could be lifted to the surface.

One Friday, weeks into the job, my close friend Leo Bowling and I were taking our turn on the bottom when Leo stopped me from my work. In his hand, he held a beautiful pearl-handled pistol.

The civilian head of North Carolina Museums, a gentleman I only remember as "Norm," had been saying for days that he would love to find such an artifact. Leo had other plans for it. He held the gun up and pointed to it, then pointed back at himself. Then he shoved it inside his jockstrap and winked at me. He was going to keep it for himself.

We'd been working for weeks with not a single day off, and when we wrapped up that day, I told Norm that we needed a break and we were going to take the weekend and we'd see him Monday morning. Well, he wouldn't have it.

There was no time for breaks, he said, and as Norm and I continued our discussion, the language we used got stronger and stronger.

Leo stepped in.

"Norm," he said, "we're going to take the weekend to rest."

And with that, he pulled out that pearl-handled pistol and placed it in Norm's hand. Norm flashed a sheepish grin and walked away. It turned out to be a great weekend.

The operation lasted about two months and we dove on ten to fifteen wrecks. Most left nothing to be salvaged, but we had a big score with the Modern Greece and smaller yields on a few others.

A handful of the wrecks were loaded with 100-pound lead bars that were to be used for molding bullets. We also found bars of tin on several wrecks. It turns out they were very valuable on the open market. After several dives that offered up plenty of tin for the state of North Carolina, Leo and I got to talking about how much money the tin was worth.

"From now on," I told Leo, "you and I will make the first dive on a wreck. If we find tin, we'll just leave it and move on to the next wreck. It'll be our bank account for one day when we need the money."

So that's what we did. After diving on all the wrecks, we'd bypassed a half dozen, calling them unsuitable for a recovery operation. Meanwhile, we made note of them on a separate chart so we could find them again. It was a perfect plan.

About a month after the operation wrapped up, state officials from North Carolina came to Washington to give a seminar, touting the success of the project. Leo and I drove up from Indian Head to attend. A large crowd packed the room where the seminar was given. Among them was Hal Waters, our pilot. When the seminar ended, Hal called me aside.

"I just want you to know that you'll be wasting your time if you go back and dive those wrecks," he said. "I went back to the ones you passed over and you'll never guess what I found. I've already cleaned them out."

I was damn near speechless.

"You cleaned out my bank account!" I said.

"It's mine now," he shot back.

We had a big laugh about it. Hal had been a volunteer, donating his time and his plane for the project, and he ended up making more money than anyone else on that job.

CLOSE CALL

D iving wasn't always fun and laughs and sunken treasure. Sometimes, it was downright dangerous.

I'd survived two major twentieth century wars. I'd stood on the deck of a ship during World War II as a Japanese kamikaze pilot pointed the nose of his disabled bomber at me. In Korea, I'd looked over the railing as a floating mine bounced into the ship but failed to explode.

I came plenty close to death on numerous occasions, but maybe the closest I ever came was in Key West, Florida, during peacetime, in a spectacularly unsuccessful attempt to test out a new diving rig developed by the Navy.

The MK-V was a mixed-gas, closed-circuit apparatus, among the first high-tech, electronically controlled diving systems. It released no bubbles to the surface, a major step forward in our field. I was among a group of EOD divers selected to test it out in open water. A quick dive, give it the thumbs up and move on. It should have been an easy day, and it would have been had I not managed to jostle the gas-mixture settings while I was getting myself into the rig.

My swim buddy Steve Bullock and I were to follow a compass course underwater to a designated location and return to the starting point. I was the navigator, but not long into the dive, I realized that something was off. I gestured to Steve, motioning around my head to let him know that I was dizzy. That's the last thing I remember.

I passed out and began floating to the surface. Steve paid it little mind. He'd misinterpreted my signal and thought that I was lost and had gone up to get my bearings. Once I broke the surface, my breathing bag dumped its gas, making me heavy, and I sank back down to Steve on my back.

Now he knew something had gone wrong and he pulled me up to the surface and called for the dive boat. By the time I'd been pulled aboard, my fingers and toes had turned blue. Blood dripped from my ears and flooded my eyes.

The next thing I remember is the terrifying sensation that I was suffocating. The corpsman held an oxygen mask over my face, but instinctively I clawed at it and fought him. He gave up, pulled off the mask and stood back as I flailed about the bottom of the boat, gasping for air.

A serious flaw in the MK-V setup was its sensitivity to rough treatment, a real problem because a Navy diver is about as rough as it gets. Because I bumped the settings while pulling on the equipment, I'd been breathing almost pure carbon monoxide and was seconds away from death. My experience prompted the Navy to take the rig back to the lab and get it right.

After surviving two wars, a test dive in Key West would have been a hell of a way to die.

DISCHARGED

By early 1964, I was a senior chief petty officer and approaching twenty years in the Navy, still at the EOD school but the enjoyment had diminished somewhat. We'd had a change of command and I didn't think too much of the new captain. I don't guess he thought much of me, either. There was no one incident, no particular falling out. Sometimes two people are like oil and water, and are never meant to co-exist.

Through some of my Navy connections, I had a civilian job waiting for me – a dream job, really – with the Naval Oceanographic Office in Suitland, Maryland. They wanted to set up a diving program for their oceanographers so they'd be Navy-qualified in their work. I'd be in charge of running that program.

And did I mention that the salary was triple what I was earning in the Navy?

Hazel and I had recently built a beautiful home set back in the woods in Southern Maryland, and we were ready to begin a new chapter of our lives.

On Valentine's Day, I reached 20 years and said goodbye to active duty. But that captain didn't send me off with a heart-shaped box of chocolates. He had to be a general nuisance one last time.

Around 11 a.m., the captain called me in to his office and told me that I'd have to return after lunch to have pictures taken because the photographer was not available. After two decades of service, I was tired of jumping through these little hoops.

"Captain," I said, "if it's all the same to you, I'd like to get my papers and be on my way."

His face turned beet red and his eyes grew wide and wild.

"Damn it," he shouted. "That's an order. Be here at 1300."

That was my last day, dealing with another officer on a power trip. It confirmed to me that I'd made the right decision. A short time later, that captain left the military and went to work in real estate. He had the audacity to call me and tell me that he had some great deals and would love to sell me some land. Some people are unbelievable.

But otherwise, I didn't give that guy another thought. The day after my discharge, I reported for work at NAVOCEANO – the military and the government are spilling over with names like this. I selected two assistants and went to work setting up a diving locker with all the equipment necessary to get the oceanographers trained and ready. We began by sending them to the Underwater Swimmers School at Key West. They returned as Navy-qualified second-class divers.

One of the reasons the office wanted its oceanographers trained as divers is because the Navy was set to partner with its British counterparts to develop an underwater test range in a deep ocean basin called Tongue of the Ocean, off the east coast of Andros Island in the Bahamas. The Atlantic Undersea Test and Evaluation Center – AUTEC, for short – became an ideal place to try out the latest underwater weaponry, rockets and torpedoes and the like. It remains in operation, though the weapons are far more advanced.

Our work commenced in mid-1964 and lasted about five years. It was a high-security project and everyone involved needed a top-secret security clearance.

Our office was responsible for carrying out surveys and recommending locations for the underwater instruments and cable routes. The cables that we were working with ran from the land out to different locations in the basin, connected to instruments that tracked the exact path of rockets and torpedoes. They also reported vital information on ocean conditions that might affect the weapons' path. The sensors could also tell you how silent your submarine was and whether it was stealthy enough to maneuver undetected.

One of our jobs involved keeping up an array of instruments moored in 1,000 fathoms of water. The instruments were at 100 feet and 150 feet down, and they had to be replaced monthly. To do so required a two-man team to make multiple dives.

Visibility in the gin-clear water stretched hundreds of feet. This was a blessing and a curse. By the time we reached the instruments, we could look up and see the dive boat floating on the surface. We could also see great masses of sharks, sometimes forty at a time, swimming in circles between us and the boat. The thought of returning to the surface was not a happy one.

To safely ascend from such depths required a decompression period of five or ten minutes at about twenty feet, where the sharks were taking up residence. While we were decompressing, the gang of sharks surrounded us, making their circles tighter and tighter until a brave one would approach slowly and nudge one of us.

The proper response, believe it or not, was to rap him on the nose with one of our tools. The shark would take off and the pack would scatter, but they'd always return and repeat the little dance.

At one point, we assigned one diver to carry a "bang stick," which is a modified 12-gauge shotgun. Instead of a trigger, it's outfitted a six-inch rod protruding from the barrel. Poke the rod against an approaching shark, the gun fires.

Only problem was that if the rod bumped against anything else — including, say, a diver — it would fire just the same. We decided the gun was a greater hazard than the sharks.

We endured only one real shark attack.

As we conducted a mini-submarine survey, my swim buddy Andy Pruna and I dove alongside the sub, filming video of the mission. We watched the mini-sub drop off a reef and disappear into darkness at 600 feet.

With the mini-sub out of sight, we started ascending through the beautiful reef and were enjoying it until Andy spotted a seven-foot nurse shark lying at the bottom of the reef. He gestured that he wanted to me to film the shark. I had a very large high-speed movie camera enclosed in a fiberglass case and I began filming as Andy swam toward the shark.

He grabbed the shark by its tail and shook it with everything he had. Next thing I know the shark is swimming straight at me, and fast. The only thing I had was the camera, so I put it between him and me. He opened wide and tore a large chunk of fiberglass out of the camera and then swam away. I was relieved, but only temporarily, because he turned and raced back at me.

Once more, I shoved that camera in his face and, once more, he took a bite out of it. When he mercifully swam away for good, I realized that as I was frozen with fright in the water, my finger was frozen on the camera's trigger. I got the entire terrifying episode on film and it remains one of my treasured keepsakes. And they say nurse sharks are harmless.

I had an equally nerve-rattling experience from the presumed safety of the mini-sub.

Let me first give the lay of the land, or rather the reef, which I described earlier. Going from the beach out to sea, you'd move across a reef to a depth of around 200 feet, at which point, there was a vertical drop-off straight down to about 1,000 feet. From there, it tapered and you could follow the floor down to a depth of about 6,000 feet. We had cables running from buildings near the beach into the water and all the way down to sets of instruments moored here at 6,000 feet.

I was along to photograph the way the cables were laying in the water, make sure everything was running as it should so we wouldn't have any unexpected problems later.

It was a two-man sub and things went well until we reached a depth of about 650 feet, still searching for the cable. That's when I heard the pilot, a guy named Casey, utter two words you never want to hear in such a situation.

"Oh, shit!"

I looked out my port and I saw the problem. We'd found the cable. It was hanging from the shallow water above to the deep water below in a long catenary, or curve. We'd managed to wedge ourselves between the taut cable and the reef. We couldn't turn in either direction, couldn't go up or down.

I was pretty certain we were screwed.

"Well, old sport," I thought. "You have had an adventurous and a happy life but it's going to end right here in this little iron coffin."

At 650 feet, we were too deep for help from the divers above, and our air would run out before anyone could organize a serious rescue effort. So we sat, silent, and waited to die. But little by little, a fraction of an inch at a time, something good was happening.

The forward momentum of the sub was stretching the cable and then that stored-up energy pushed us back. As we began slowly backing down, the wire eased up and off our bow. We were free.

"What do you say we call it a day?" Casey said.

I tried to speak but couldn't make a single word come out of my mouth. I nodded in the affirmative.

After construction at AUTEC was completed, our work there wasn't done. We returned each year to conduct a beach survey out to a depth of fifty feet to determine whether all the action at the site was leaving environmental damage. We surveyed the sand and vegetation, checking for any changes, and we studied the underwater coral to be sure that it remained healthy.

I enjoyed heading back there each year, and Hazel didn't mind, either, because after our work wrapped up, she often flew down to meet me in Nassau, where the project had its headquarters. We'd linger in the Bahamas a few days, sometimes longer, enjoying each other's company and soaking up the island culture.

During the day, we'd lay around on the beach, maybe go boating or diving or spearfishing, maybe all of the above. After dark, we'd get dressed up and find a nightclub.

We made many friends in Nassau over the years. One of them, Ray Moore, let us stay in his waterfront apartment for two weeks while he and his wife vacationed in Europe. All we had to do was take care of their cat. I found myself thinking even more how I could get used to life in a tropical paradise.

But we weren't quite ready for that yet. In fact, as it turned out, I had one more war left in me.

VIETNAM

Heading home from one of our Nassau vacations, Hazel and I stopped to change planes in Miami. We were killing time in the airport when a particular display stopped me in my tracks. It was a boat, a tiny boat. The sign said it was called an Aqua Dart, and it turned out to be a predecessor to the Jet Ski.

This early version didn't have a jet pump, so it had a 25-horsepower Mercury outboard motor jutting out beneath the hull. There was only room for a rider's body from the waist up, stretched out on an aluminum plate attached to the rear of the vessel.

An advertisement boasted that it could do 50 miles per hour over the water. I picked up some of the material to read on the plane. I was fascinated and thinking how much fun it would be to ride, how badly I wanted one.

Back at work, I settled in to tackle the backlog of paperwork that had accumulated on my desk. Paperwork was never my favorite thing, but on this day I came across a document requesting input for a better way to survey the rivers and canals in Vietnam, where the United States had become involved in a difficult and increasingly unpopular war.

The Navy had been attempting to do it with large survey boats, carrying a crew of eight people, and one of those boats had recently been lost, along with everyone on board, while attempting to survey the Mekong River Delta. They needed a faster, safer way to survey.

My mind drifted back to Miami and the Aqua Dart. I started scheming. If it could be equipped with a high-speed depth sounder and some navigation equipment, a high-quality survey would require only one person.

We'd been working with a new 350-degree panoramic camera that had once been used on submarines' periscopes to photograph enemy harbors, and that too was perfect for this project. If it was mounted on the Aqua Dart, the camera could snap photographs that would help the Navy pinpoint locations and landmarks.

I put together an official proposal and strongly suggested that the only people capable of carrying out such missions were UDT members. The next thing I knew I was authorized to proceed with the project and given all the funds I needed.

I ordered four Aqua Darts from the inventor, who was building them in his garage in Perry, New York. No matter, it was a fine product. Once we received them, we installed the cameras and the high-speed depth sounders. We took them out on the Potomac River for trial runs and everything worked according to plan.

Lieutenant Commander Bob Condon, the head of Underwater Demolition Team 11, visited and after trying one out, he was hooked. He loved the idea but suggested there might be a problem. The waters they'd be navigating in Vietnam were strewn with floating logs and debris and the Aqua Dart wouldn't last long with the prop sticking out of the bottom of the craft unprotected.

After some thought, we installed two stainless steel runners beneath the hull, hoping it would be enough to shield the prop from peril. A few days later, we sent Condon photos of us going over not only logs, but also over ski jumps in the Potomac River.

We were back in business.

We met him and his team in Needles, California, for a more advanced tryout. On the first day, the team surveyed a section of the

Colorado River. Then we developed the film and constructed a chart that included water depths. I felt like I'd gone back in time, back working with UDT.

The team was preparing to rotate into Vietnam and the commander asked if I'd be interested in bringing the equipment along for use under wartime conditions. One last chance for an adventure with the Navy.

I wasted no time pulling together all the gear for the trip. I hired an assistant, a guy by the name of Joe Gatone. He'd been working for the Department of Fish & Wildlife and needed a change. Joe wasn't a military guy, but he had an electronics background and he'd be a good man to keep up the cameras and the depth sounders. I hired him on the condition that he'd go to Vietnam with me. In a war zone, I told him, we'd be authorized to draw maximum overtime. He liked that.

Hazel wasn't crazy about the idea, but she knew that when I got excited about something, it was hard to slow me down. She went along with it, but it didn't take long for her to regret it.

We left for Saigon in December 1967 with Joe and me on one flight and all our equipment on another, but when we arrived we found that one box hadn't made it. I wired the office, informing them that I'd arrived but some of the gear was missing.

Somehow the message got confused because they turned around and called Hazel, telling her that I was missing in Vietnam. For the next several days, she was a wreck, wondering what happened, wondering where I was and if I was dead or alive.

When later I located the lost equipment and wired the office with the good news, they in turn informed Hazel that, hallelujah, I'd been found, safe and sound.

As we were loading the chopper in Saigon, bound for the Mekong Delta, one of the Navy guys asked whether we wanted weapons and I, of course, replied that I absolutely wanted a gun. I think Joe was starting to get shaken at this point. I knew he'd never been in the military, but I began to doubt if he'd ever fired a gun.

He shook his head. No, he wouldn't be requiring a weapon.

The Navy had a barracks ship anchored in the lower section of the Mekong River. The team was there when we arrived. For our work area, they'd tied a barge to the side of the ship. Our gear was on it, waiting for us.

It was a good setup, with one small exception. Each night the current washed great masses of water plants and driftwood toward the barge and it collected along the bow, along with plenty of snakes and lizards, many of which seemed bigger than me. Each morning, over a cup of coffee, I stood at the rail of the barge and watched the crew clear out the critters that had crawled aboard. But there was always one that would sneak up later and startle you.

Over the next few days, the Aqua Darts made a couple of runs down the river, once being dropped in from a boat and once being dropped from a chopper. Everything was going as planned, except for one thing. I was noticing some tension between Condon and his executive officer. At the time, I couldn't put my finger on it. Later, I'd find out.

The weekend rolled around and we were taking it easy with nothing to do. Condon stopped by to talk and told me that the next day, a Sunday, they were going to take some troops upriver and put them ashore. He asked if I wanted to come along.

No, I told him. I had a good book going and I figured I'd stick right there and maybe finish it off.

The next morning, he climbed aboard a flame-thrower boat, known as a Zippo. Heavy armor, three or four inches of steel, surrounded the cabin.

It wasn't enough.

The boat returned later without him and those aboard brought word that Bob Condon had been killed.

As the boat rounded a curve in the river, a Viet Cong fighter fired a rocket-propelled grenade from the shore. The RPG penetrated the thick steel and tore down Condon where he stood.

He was a good man and his passing knocked the wind out of me. It also did not escape me that once again my life had been spared in a moment that could have gone either way. It had been his day to die, not mine.

After Condon's death, I learned the source of the tension I'd sensed between him and his executive officer. That XO assumed command of the team and a few days later he informed me that he'd allow no further tests of the Aqua Dart. Too dangerous, he said. So the team went back to risking the lives of eight men instead of one, and I began planning to make my way home.

I had damn poor timing.

We awoke the next morning to the sound of gunfire and bombing. I'd managed to get myself caught in the middle of the Tet Offensive, the largest battle of the Vietnam War.

I told Joe to pack his bag. We were clearing out. It was no place for a civilian and at that time, it was no place for me, either.

As the fighting intensified, it began to sink in how serious this was. We jumped on a boat headed over to the nearby airstrip and found American troops placing bags over the heads of North Vietnamese prisoners of war, lining them up and loading them onto planes. I made a beeline for the office.

"My name is Mr. Bright," I told the guy in charge. "I'm here on a classified mission and I must get back to Washington immediately."

The urgency of the situation must not have been sufficiently conveyed because he responded that, unless I was a POW, there was no seat for me on that plane, nor was it likely that we could get out of there at all that day.

We took a seat in his office and waited. And waited. Much later that day, we were still perched in our seats when I was informed that two spots were available on a soon-to-depart aircraft bound for an airstrip north of Saigon. We jumped up and climbed aboard, happy to be starting our journey home.

When we landed at the airstrip, I spotted an Army colonel sitting in a jeep and I fed him the same line of bull about my classified mission and how it was imperative that we get back to Washington.

The only thing moving that night was the general's chopper, he said, and I responded that it would suit just fine. Later the general tracked me down and told me that conditions were bad in Saigon, violent and dangerous. He recommended we sit tight until morning, when he would send his pilot to deliver us.

The general was true to his word and the next morning his pilot welcomed us aboard. From the skies above Saigon, we peered down on the street warfare. Upon landing at Tan Son Nhat airport, I hurried to the military desk and recited the same story that had worked twice before.

"We haven't had a plane leave in two days," the man at the desk said, "and I doubt if there will be one today."

"Well," I said, "just in case, we'll be sitting right here."

Luck shined on us again because that afternoon, a plane did take off, bound for Bangkok, and we were on it.

My project had been spiked, I'd failed to achieve my goal and I was going home, a victim of war and politics. Not much you can do about that, except make the best of it.

In Bangkok, I found a phone and called Hazel. I told her about my great escape – and my great idea.

"Meet me in Paris," I said.

We spent two weeks in France, Spain and Italy. My job may not have gone according to plan, but I survived another war and made a trip around the world in the process.

ARCTIC

Having spent plenty of time diving in the tropics, I wasn't too sure when, in 1971, I was approached about a new assignment, in a place that was decidedly not tropical.

The Arctic.

I hesitated, given that I'm the type of guy who still shivers at the thought of wintertime in Boston. The cold has never been my thing, but no doubt that this would be an adventure. I was in.

The assignment was to explore the feasibility of using SCUBA divers to study the characteristics of the underside of Arctic sea ice. In November of that year, we flew to Point Barrow, Alaska, for orientation dives. The temperature was 10 degrees and we had only five hours of useful daylight, but we made the most of it. Using a gas-powered auger, we cut holes through a foot of ice and descended into the frigid waters. After a couple of days getting acclimated, we were ready to go and we boarded a plane from Alaska bound for T-3, a floating ice island 285 miles from the North Pole.

Since the 1950s, the Defense Department had been sponsoring all sorts of research on T-3 and there was a steady rotation of scientists and military types coming and going between Alaska and this kidney-shaped frozen island.

Peering out the window of our airplane at the dark, icy wasteland, I began to wonder if maybe this was not the smartest thing I'd ever done. Stepping for the first time onto the ice did nothing to change my perspective. The temperature was 30 below and the wind so strong that it might have knocked over a smaller man.

I wondered how people lived like this. Some researchers there were on their second or third two-year stint. I imagined that life on T-3 had to mess with a man's head after a while.

After landing, that thought was confirmed. I was escorted to my living quarters, a heated facility that was not entirely unpleasant. That is, until I noticed the chalk outline of a body near my bed. There had been a murder on T-3.

A few weeks earlier, a fight broke out among a couple of workers, drunk on raisin wine they'd made. One of the men pulled a knife. The fight didn't last long after that.

It was surreal to fly to the top of the world and find myself bunking in the middle of a crime scene. Then again, this was a surreal place. It was always dark. A slight glow moved along the horizon over the course of the day, but it wasn't enough to illuminate anything. The moon stayed directly overhead, traveling in a tight circle as the day progressed.

The cold didn't bother me near as much as I'd feared. We were well stocked with Arctic-appropriate clothing and heaters hummed everywhere we went. The strangest thing was using the bathroom. An oil heater kept the small outhouse more than toasty, around 100 degrees, but when you lifted the toilet lid, the Arctic air came rushing in. I'll just say this, you didn't linger long over that hole.

We spent seven days at T-3 and the diving was extraordinary. A previous generation of researchers had drilled a hole, six feet in diameter, down through thirty feet of ice to provide an entry point into the water and a heated hut stood over the hole to prevent it from freezing over. It was from there that we began our excursions.

We called it "The Old Ice Hole" and descending those thirty feet was like traveling down into a well, but when you broke free into open water it was incredible. The water depth at that time was about 1,000 feet and it amazed me how much marine life thrived in 28-degree waters.

In addition to measuring and charting the area, we surveyed the underside of the ice and found many stalactites that had formed there just as they form in caves in the earth. We measured and photographed them, and took samples back to the surface. We also retrieved many unknown specimens that we handed over to the biologist to study.

Americans had been doing research on T-3 since the early 1950s and it had been an invaluable site for studying the Arctic, but a few years after our trip, operations there were shut down and the island was abandoned.

The ice was slowly disappearing. It was no longer safe. In the coming decades, T-3 drifted into the Atlantic Ocean and melted away.

LAST JOB

My last major job with the oceanographic office began when my boss, Ed Ridley, called me in to vent about problems he was having extracting core samples from harbors around the United States.

Core samples can provide a wealth of information on any number of things, from weather trends to the history of the earth. In this case, Ridley's group was out to study pollution in the harbors, to gauge the damage caused by years of discharges from industrial plants and shipyards. They were looking for heavy metals, such as mercury, anything that could be harmful to humans.

Core samples are taken by driving a pipe deep into the earth. Inside the pipe is a plastic liner, and when that liner is removed, the core of the earth comes up with it, ready to be extracted and studied.

They'd been trying to take the core samples with oceanographic ships, but the harbor waters were shallow and they couldn't generate enough force with their coring tubes to penetrate to the required depth.

"Hell, Ed, I can do that," I told him. "This is no problem at all for divers."

I began to lay out my plan. All it would take, I explained, was a couple of guys and a small boat. We'd dive to the bottom and use something like a pile driver to plunge the core pipe into the bottom, then run a line from the pipe back up to the bow of the boat, where we'd use a winch to pull the samples to the surface.

Ed looked at me, half smiling, shaking his head.

"You're making this up as you go, aren't you?"

"Certainly."

"You've got the job."

When I told the idea to my good friend Bob Guthery, he didn't hesitate at all and agreed to join me. We rented a U-Haul truck and hooked an 18-foot Boston Whaler boat to the tow hitch. In the truck, we piled in all of our tools and equipment, as well as camping gear. We strung two hammocks across the back and that truck was our home for the next two months. We made a pretty penny by pocketing all the money we'd been given to pay for hotels during our journey.

My plan worked like a charm. At each harbor, we'd crank the winch and up would come a pristine core sample. We stashed the eight-foot long tubes that contained them in the nearest walk-in freezer, usually inside a base mess hall where food was kept. Before leaving for the next harbor, we packed each sample in dry ice and shipped them back to the office.

Our trip began in Baltimore, then proceeded to Norfolk, Virginia; Jacksonville and Tampa in Florida; Mobile, Alabama; and New Orleans, Louisiana; before heading west and finishing up in California with stops at San Diego, Hunter's Point, Oakland and Vallejo.

Three days was all it took in each place to get the job done, though on occasion we had to stay longer if there were equipment troubles or bad weather or if the night life was good.

PEACE & PLENTY

As a teenager in Texas, it was Hollywood's propaganda films romanticizing the Navy that gave me my first nudge toward a sailor's life. The real thing wasn't quite how it was portrayed on the big screen, but it was still pretty great, a life choice I have never once regretted.

Many years later, Hollywood got me again, this time with a television program called "Adventures in Paradise." A Korean War veteran by the name of Adam Troy, played by Gardner McKay, never left the Pacific after the war ended. Instead, he captained a schooner named "Tiki III" and sailed every bit of that ocean, blown by the wind from one adventure to the next, the whole thing set to the beat of island music.

The show lasted three years and ninety-one episodes. I don't believe I missed a single one.

I'd caught the travel bug during World War II, but this show sealed the deal for me. I wanted Adam Troy's life, or something very close to it. Throughout the 1960s, I preoccupied myself with this dream, scheming ways to turn it into reality, scheming ways to persuade Hazel to go along.

At most any Navy base in the country, the recreation program supplies sailboats that can be rented on the cheap and over the years I'd become quite competent. I'd worked my way up from the small ones to the larger ones.

In Indian Head, in addition to the ski boat and later a cabin cruiser that I'd rebuilt in the back yard, I scraped together a few bucks and bought an old Chesapeake Bay skipjack. And when I say it was old, it was built in 1916. It was called the Katy Rowe and it was the first large sailboat I owned. I cut my teeth on that boat, but traded it in for a twenty-eight-foot cruiser while I began work on my big dream: my own sailboat, built by my own hands.

In 1970, I dropped about twelve thousand dollars and ordered the hull and cabin of a thirty-four-foot Seafarer sloop, the bare skeleton that would become so much more, the sailboat that would be my "Tiki III," the vessel that would turn me into Adam Troy, sailing the seas and chasing adventure.

Hazel thought I was half-crazy – or fully crazy, depending on the day – but in the back yard of our house in the woods, I set myself to building that dream. I spent every spare minute turning that shell of a boat into something wonderful. Most evenings I worked until midnight. A long extension cord ran to an outlet on the back deck of the house, and often it was Hazel who decided when I'd worked long enough. She'd open the back door, step outside and yank out the power cord, leaving me sitting in the dark.

I began by fashioning the inside of the cabin, building bunks and installing the cabinetry and all the other furnishings from the cook stove to the head. Then I moved on to the deck, where I installed the rails and the rigging and all the outside woodwork. I bought a second-hand engine and did all the work installing it.

I'd never attempted anything like this and I made some expensive mistakes, but I also learned a lot. After two years, almost to the day, my boat was ready for the water.

"Peace & Plenty" was the name I chose. It came from a book I'd read on Bahamian history. During the Revolutionary War, many British loyalists in the American colonies didn't believe in the cause and chose to leave, rather than get caught up in the fighting.

In South Carolina, a plantation owner by the name of Rolle dismantled his mansion brick by brick and loaded it, along with all of his belongs and all of his slaves, aboard a ship called the Peace & Plenty.

Rolle carried it all to Great Exuma Island in the Bahamas, where he started anew. I kept a copy of the account in the forward compartment of the boat. Most of all, it struck me as a neat name for my new masterpiece.

The maiden voyage of my Peace & Plenty came in July 1972. We carried her aboard a low-boy truck south about twenty miles to the Aqua-Land Marina on the Potomac River. In the shadow of the Harry Nice Bridge connecting Southern Maryland to the northern neck of Virginia, we put the Peace & Plenty on the water and sprinkled a little champagne over the bow. No sense wasting a bottle by smashing it on the boat.

Joining Hazel and me were our daughter Andie and son-in-law Jim Corby, as well as our oldest grandson, Brent. Jim was set to graduate that day from the University of Maryland, but he opted to skip the ceremony and have his diploma mailed to him, so he could be there for the first excursion.

The plan was to take the boat down the Potomac and into the Chesapeake Bay, where we'd keep it at a marina on Solomon's Island. That day, we went as far as Tall Timbers, a calm inlet on the river, before continuing on the next day.

It was on this trip that I discovered that the engine, the secondhand motor, was not going to do the job. We sailed straight into a strong storm that wasted no time blowing the Peace & Plenty ashore. It was a sandy bank and no harm was done.

The engine was not stronger than the wind, not powerful enough to keep us offshore. First outing, first lesson learned. But man, what a great feeling to be behind the wheel.

ISLAMORADA

Between the new sailboat and the motor boats we'd had, we were well immersed in the boating lifestyle. Weekends were our time to be on the water, and over the years we had a lot of great days out on the Potomac or the Chesapeake, swimming and waterskiing and sometimes camping on the beaches.

It was almost perfect, except for one thing: Summers were too short. The climate in Maryland gives you a healthy dose of all four seasons, but I only ever had any use for one of them.

On our many trips to the Bahamas, Hazel and I talked about buying a place and moving to the islands. Problem was the government there was so unstable that you didn't know what would happen next. It was a nice thought, but not realistic.

Hazel retired from her federal job in the early 1970s and she was quite content to tag along with me to jobs in the Bahamas, Key West and the like, turning them into little vacations once the work was done.

And so she did in Key West in 1973. After a few days of rest and relaxation, we started for home. Driving north through the Keys, we spotted a new housing development, Venetian Shores, popping up in Islamorada. We decided to take a spin through the neighborhood.

It was, or at least would become, a classic Florida Keys housing development. The area was made up of more than a dozen streets, each filled with lots that backed up to canals, which led out to the wider Snake Creek, which led out to the Florida Bay on one side and on the other, the open Atlantic Ocean.

It had the makings of a beautiful place, but on that day, it was pretty bare. Most of the lots were vacant and the place was peppered with "for sale" signs. We drove through, street by street, debating the merits of each lot, our conversation growing more serious.

Hazel favored an end lot on Snake Creek because it would offer the best view of open water. But I had to explain to her that the heavy boat traffic on the creek would be noisy and bothersome, creating constant wakes that would lap at our dock and damage any boat tied up to it.

It'd be a better bet, I told her, to find a nice lot on a quiet canal. And then we found such a spot. It had a great water view and was far enough down a canal that we'd never have problems with boat wakes or rough water. We had talked ourselves into it.

We found a phone and dialed the realtor, who promised that he'd take care of us first thing in the morning since it was nearly closing time at the office. But we were only passing through. I told him if we couldn't meet that day, we couldn't meet at all.

Stay put, he said, and before long he met us and led us back to his home. He lived in the development, too. We sat down at his table and worked out the details over dinner. We paid $17,000 for the lot, a fair down payment for the new life we'd been dreaming about.

With the papers signed and the deal done, we continued back to Maryland but my heart and my mind never really left the Keys. From that day on, all I could think about was building a house on our new lot, getting down there and tying up the Peace & Plenty on our very own dock. There was no real rush, but I was in a big damn hurry.

The economy was bad and, at the office, the word on everyone's mind was downsizing. It didn't scare me. I welcomed it, hoped for it. Once again, I had a friend in the right place and he promised to do for me what he could.

There was one condition, he said. I couldn't tell Hazel who did it, in case she got mad.

I got the call a few weeks later while in San Diego for work. My friend told me that my job had been abolished and I was eligible to retire with full benefits. I was forty-eight years old and free. I called Hazel and when I told her that my job had been abolished, the line went silent.

After a moment, she said, "I know what you pulled off!"

She wasn't mad, not really. But I think she realized then that a big change was coming to our lives, and it was coming fast.

With the USS Sampson in Lima, Peru, in 1943

Aboard the USS Chilton in China in 1949

New member of Underwater Demolition Team 1 in 1950

Hazel and Chet Bright on their wedding day in 1958

Diving with a camera at the Atlantic Undersea Test and Evaluation Center,
off Andros Island in the Bahamas in 1965

In Vietnam for the Naval Oceanographic Office in 1968

Preparing for an Arctic dive in 1970

Building the Peace & Plenty in the early 1970s

Islamorada house in the 1980s

**With Marina Gibson
on Crooked Island, Bahamas**

Hazel Bright eating lunch aboard the Peace & Plenty in the Bahamas

Aboard the Peace & Plenty

**Swallowing the anchor
on Cobb Island, Maryland, in 2009**

PART TWO

A NEW LIFE

A s Hazel and I loaded the Peace & Plenty to begin the journey to our new home, I could hardly believe how much had happened in the months since we stopped in Islamorada on a whim.

We'd bought a waterfront lot in the Florida Keys and commenced construction on a home. I'd retired from my job with the National Oceanographic Office and was, for the first time since before World War II, blissfully unemployed.

We'd sold our home in Maryland and much of what was in it. The new owners agreed to take our aging German shepherd, Gypsy. She was quite old, struggled to move and was not up for the trip. The rest of our possessions we'd loaded into a moving truck and sent to storage in Miami. I'd driven our car down to Florida, taking a Greyhound bus back, so a vehicle would be waiting for us when we got there.

On the day we set sail from Maryland, bound for the Keys in June 1974, my life had been stripped to its bare essentials: Hazel and the Peace & Plenty. We'd taken the boat on some weekend trips in the Chesapeake Bay, but this would be our first extended outing, our first trip down the Intracoastal Waterway, an easily navigable stretch of water spanning most of the eastern seaboard.

It offers an ideal alternative to traveling on the open Atlantic, and the various towns along the route make it perfect for a leisurely sail. We were in no rush. We'd decided in advance that if we liked a place, we'd stop and take it all in before continuing down the waterway.

Our trip did not get off to a pleasant start. We'd gone only twenty miles when a crab trap wrapped itself around our propeller, making a tangled mess of the chicken wire from which the trap was constructed. The only way to rectify the situation was to jump in the water and get to work. It wouldn't have been a problem, except for the jellyfish. At that time of year, the bay belongs to the jellyfish. You swim at your own risk. I had no choice. Into the water I went.

In the twenty minutes it took me to free the remnants of the crab trap from the propeller, the jellyfish had their way with me. My body was on fire when I climbed back aboard the boat.

Not much can be done to alleviate the pain from a jellyfish attack, so I did the first thing that came to mind. I grabbed a half-filled bottle of rum, sat down and drank every last drop. I couldn't say whether the stinging had run its course or if the rum had blocked out my pain. Either way, I was feeling fine.

In Norfolk, at the southern end of the Chesapeake Bay, we met a congressman and his family traveling in a large, powerful houseboat with two engines. We chatted them up and discovered that they were also headed for the Keys. We departed Norfolk a day before they did, but a couple days later they overtook us, waving and shouting that they'd see us in the Keys.

We'd see them sooner than that. When we arrived in Morehead City, North Carolina, I spotted the houseboat – on land. The good congressman had run aground and bent both props, requiring it to be hauled out of the water for repairs.

Hazel and I stayed overnight and continued south the next morning. Sure enough, a few days later, they passed us again. We caught up to them at Southport, along the Cape Fear River.

It was like the race of the tortoise and the hare. I was beginning to think our little sailboat was going to beat that powerful vessel to the Keys, but they took off and kept going and got there well ahead of us.

We were taking our sweet time and having a great time. As we crossed the Florida line, I sat at the wheel and began to feel that the end of our journey was close. Aside from the crab trap incident, things had gone smoothly.

"I've always heard stories about people running aground in the waterway," I told Hazel. "You would have to be deaf, dumb and blind to run aground in it."

The very next morning I was sitting at the wheel, half asleep, not paying attention to my job, and ran hard aground. The site of my embarrassment was north of St. Augustine. I'd run aground on a falling tide, at nearly high tide. Nothing to do but wait for the next high tide to lift the Peace & Plenty from the bottom.

We made ourselves comfortable. I put out a couple of anchors to keep the boat sitting straight up and made the best of a bad situation by hopping out and scrubbing the bottom of the boat.

When the tide returned and lifted us up, we eased on into the marina at St. Augustine. Overnight dockage at most marinas at that time cost eight or ten dollars, but at St. Augustine it was free. Next to the marina was a band shell, and it being Saturday night we were treated to a free concert as we sat on the boat, sipping a cocktail under a full moon.

I looked at Hazel and said, "We have truly arrived in paradise."

Days later we began to notice the wealth in South Florida. Each waterfront home was bigger and more beautiful than the last, and Hazel spent the entire day on the deck, marveling at the houses and snapping pictures.

Arriving in Fort Lauderdale, we decided to celebrate and pulled into the most expensive marina in town, the Pier 66, which was filled with large, lavish yachts.

For thirty-five dollars a night, they gave us the VIP treatment and did everything they could to please us. It was above and beyond anything we had ever experienced.

The next night we docked at Miami Marina and paid $3.50 for the night. Back in those days, the marinas were subsidized by the city, which kept the price down. Now, nearly four decades later, the cost runs about a hundred dollars per night.

Two days later, we sailed into Snake Creek, eased down a canal and tied up the Peace & Plenty to the dock in front of our new home, which was months away from completion.

The trip lasted two months. Hazel enjoyed every bit of it, but as we reached Islamorada, she didn't have much to say. I think it was all sinking in. I'd taken her out of her beautiful home deep in the woods of Southern Maryland and dragged her all the way to Florida to some pile of rocks in the middle of the ocean.

Only one house had been built on our street. I spent a lot of time telling her how wonderful this place would look in a few years, when the neighborhood was finished.

At that moment, I suspect she would have been happier had we waited a few years to move south, but our early arrival turned out to be a blessing. She was able to supervise the completion of the house, making decisions on all the finish work and the decorating, and I was able to start on the landscaping outside. In short order, we had our dream house with the Peace & Plenty tied up out back.

Before long, we both agreed: It was paradise.

DIVE BOATS

As we settled in to life in the Keys, I spent much of my time exploring, getting to know the people and the waters around the island. I was out diving every chance I got, and I'd found all of the beautiful reefs in the area and a few of the local shipwrecks. So when I was offered a job as captain of a dive boat, I was well qualified to show the tourists a good time.

For the better part of a year, I captained the boat and took the visitors to some fun, local spots. But most of them weren't experienced divers and the job got to be a drag, the same thing day after day.

I left when I was offered the same job on a twenty-five-passenger, eighty-five-foot boat with twin International diesel engines. I got this job much the same way I first got into UDT so many years ago, replacing a dead man. The captain of boat had died in a diving accident and on my second day of work, I took his family and friends out to sea to conduct a funeral and scatter his ashes.

That same week, the captain who took over my job on the six-passenger boat lost a tourist diver. Diving in the Keys was apparently a lot more hazardous than the diving I'd been doing for the previous twenty-five years.

The new boat was called Hi There, after a favorite expression of the woman who owned it. I hated the name, but the boat was a beauty. I had a former Coast Guardsman for a mate and a little hippie girl for a cook. Mostly we chartered for dive clubs from states east of the Mississippi, and we took them to places like Dry Tortugas and the Bahamas. It was a great opportunity for me to learn about places that I'd later sail to aboard the Peace & Plenty.

Beautiful reefs are everywhere around those islands and few people ever experience diving on them. Most of the club members wanted to sightsee, but a lot of them were underwater photographers and carried thousands of dollars' worth of equipment. Some were there to spearfish and others hunted for lobster, but as a rule they were more competent than the tourists I'd been chauffeuring around in the tiny six-passenger boat, which made the job much more pleasant.

A favorite spot was Cay Sal Banks, a group of islands not far from Cuba that belong to the Bahamas. The place was loaded with stunning reefs and an abundance of sea life.

You could be diving in ten feet of water and then come upon a "blue hole," an area 600-feet deep, the size of a football field and pocked with caves that divers could swim into and explore.

Cay Sal Island employed a customs man named John, and at the start of each trip I'd check in with him. He'd count the passengers and collect five dollars for each before giving me clearance papers that allowed us to be in the area for a given period. He had three Bahamian helpers, who never seemed to do anything more than sit in the shade of a palm tree.

To keep things running smooth, I'd bring John a bottle of Scotch each time we made a trip, until one day he told me that he'd given up drinking. After that, I'd bring him ice cream. This went on for months until he informed me that he'd given up quitting drinking.

It was back to Scotch.

ICE

Those first years living in the Keys weren't always happy for Hazel. I was often out running around on the charter boats and she never quite felt at home.

She joined every volunteer group or neighborhood club she could find in order to keep herself busy – the Red Cross, the Gray Ladies at the hospital, a book club, a sewing club and plenty more that I can't recall – but she wasn't getting much out of life.

I'd grown tired of the charter business myself, so I gave my notice to the owner of Hi There. She accepted it without much of a fuss. She'd been dating a young man who had a captain's license and she installed him in my job. He made one trip out and returned to the dock to fuel up, only he filled the tank with regular gas instead of diesel fuel. Needless to say, he destroyed the engines. The owner had no insurance and that was the end of her charter business.

I'd been itching to do some exploring aboard my own boat and Hazel needed something to snap her out of her rut, so I suggested a trip to the Bahamas, where we had many friends from our working days. She loved the idea.

By the early 1970s, I'd spent no small amount of time in the Bahamas, for work and for pleasure, and I'd devoured book after book about the islands and their waters. I had, to this point, never attempted to sail there myself. But from the books, I'd learned that the winds on that route will, almost without fail, die down after sunset, making for an easy passage.

Hazel and I planned our departure around that basic fact, electing to sail to Miami and make the fifty-mile jump from Miami to Bimini, the westernmost point in the Bahamas, under the big moon and bright stars. We'd sail along at five knots, which would put us into Bimini after about ten hours.

The trip had been planned for some time and by the first of May, we were sure that the last strong winds coming from the north had blown themselves out, and good weather had settled in. We spent a day at Miami Marina and motored out late in the afternoon. The two-cylinder Volvo diesel engine was running as smooth as a two cylinder could run, though as a rule, they don't run all that smooth. Still, they are sure dependable.

By the time the sun sank over the horizon, the wind was already betraying us. Instead of lying down, as all the books insisted it would, the wind was picking up, gaining strength by the minute. The smart thing to do would have been to turn around, but we'd been planning this trip to the islands for too long. We were not turning back.

Instead, we were motor sailing with the main sail up to steady the boat and keep it from rolling too much. When we hit the open sea, Hazel retired to her bunk and I stayed topside to keep an eye on things. The wind never did let up. It got stronger and stronger as the night went on.

A compass and a radio direction finder were the only instruments I had to guide us. I would have given anything to know how fast we were traveling. An RDF can help you zero in on your location, but as the wind increased so did the salt spray and it was too wet and windy to play with the RDF. I had to be satisfied to know that we were moving through the water.

My first hint that we were not traveling at the desired pace came when a patch of seaweed floated along the side of the boat. If we were making good time, we'd move right past the seaweed and keep sailing. Instead, the seaweed seemed to lay there alongside us forever before lazily drifting off. We were making headway, but not much.

When at last the sun appeared, I saw whitecaps in all directions, but no land anywhere. Hazel crawled out of her bunk long enough to take the wheel for a bit and allow me to go below and take some radio bearings. I wished I hadn't.

They told me that after sailing all night long, we were only halfway to Bimini. We'd been doing merely two or three knots. I grabbed a cup of coffee and a quick bite to eat then went back to the wheel. Hazel returned to her bunk.

I fought the wind all day and we pulled into Bimini in late afternoon. I'd been up for twenty-four hours to make fifty miles.

After a few days' rest – and a bit of partying – we headed across the Great Bahama Bank to Chub Cay. There we anchored in with several other boats while the strong winds continued to blow.

One brave man decided to try for Nassau and pulled out the next morning. He returned, battered, after a few hours. Everything on his boat was soaked and he was lamenting that a big main sail he'd kept stored in a bag on the deck had disappeared into the water. It was not the day to go to Nassau.

We held tight for a few days and stocked up on food and supplies. I donned my diving gear, plunged into the water and came back loaded with fish, conch and lobster. I'd installed a small refrigerator and freezer, so it was packed and we had all we could eat for some time.

When we next awoke to a day with a light breeze, we sailed over to Nassau without incident. It was great to be back in the place where we'd enjoyed so many pleasant vacations and met so many fine people. We visited old friends, took in the nighttime attractions and enjoyed life.

Things were going great until one morning I attempted to start the engine, with the intention of using it to charge the battery for the fridge. The starter failed. The wiring inside it had burned out.

This wasn't the worst thing in the world since I could also crank-start the engine, but that starter doubled as a generator. Without it, we could not recharge the battery for the refrigerator and freezer. No shop existed in Nassau with the capability of fixing our problem.

On my own, I wouldn't have worried about this at all. A refrigerator was a luxury, but it was a luxury to which Hazel had become accustomed.

I explained to her that we were one of the few sailboats that had a fridge. Most did without it and made do just fine. With all the seafood I could catch, it would be no hardship.

She was not pleased, but being such a wonderful lady and knowing how much I'd wanted to make this trip around the islands, she bit her tongue and didn't make much of a fuss.

Before leaving Nassau, I purchased a small block of ice, but it was gone in no time. We were loaded with canned goods and dry stores, so we were happy and eating well. But I should have known it wouldn't last.

We lounged around on the beautiful beaches of uninhabited islands for a couple weeks until one day, Hazel became almost hysterical. She'd been holding back but could do it no longer.

"I have simply got to have a glass of iced tea or iced water or iced … something," she said. "I've got to have some ice."

It might seem a little odd to get so worked up about something so simple as ice, but I knew that this wasn't something she was going to let pass. I had to figure out a way to get the woman some ice.

We'd planned to leave the next morning for Rum Cay, and I told her – though I knew it not to be true – that there was sure to be a store there where we could get ice.

Rum Cay was a beautiful island that had been named Santa Maria de la Concepcion when it was encountered by Christopher Columbus in October 1492. Its current name was derived from the wreck of a West Indian ship loaded with, you guessed it, rum. At one time, it had been a prosperous place, benefitting from the export of salt to Nova Scotia until a hurricane destroyed the salt pans beyond repair. Then for some years they exported pineapples and cattle, but the place came upon hard times and the population fell, by some estimates, to less than seventy-five people. We found an island more populated by donkeys than humans.

From the minute we anchored, I was on a mission to find ice. I left Hazel aboard the boat and jumped into the dinghy, headed for shore with my small Igloo cooler, just in case. I knocked on the first door I came to and asked if there was any ice to be had on the island. A man there told me that the commissioner of the island was one of the few in possession of a generator and if I were to have any luck at all, it would be through him.

I located the commissioner's home and found him most hospitable. I explained my particular situation, upon which he excused himself. He returned with two trays of ice, courtesy of his government-issued deep freeze, and dumped them into my cooler.

He instructed me to return the following day for more.

"What's this going to cost me?" I asked.

"Don't worry about it," he said. "You can pay me for both batches tomorrow."

I started to get an uneasy feeling, but I also figured that if my marriage was going to continue, Hazel had to have ice.

The following day, I returned and picked up two more trays' worth and a small plastic container of ice.

"How much?" I asked again.

"Ten dollars," he said.

A steep price, but Hazel got her ice. And I stayed married.

THE CARIBBEAN

Haiti

After a few years of making the short hop across to the Bahamas and exploring its islands, I began to feel the pull of the deeper Caribbean. We'd been to many of the places there but never had the luxury of time to wander and spend lazy days immersing ourselves in the exotic cultures.

Hazel required little convincing. From her hesitant start, she'd become a capable and enthusiastic sailor. We provisioned the Peace & Plenty in November 1980 for a six-month trip, made loose plans for the course we'd follow and then we set sail.

We crossed to the Bahamas, made our way down to Great Inagua Island, the southernmost district in the Bahamian chain of islands, and then prepared for an overnight run to Haiti. We got underway after dark and set a course for Cap du Mole on the northwest corner of the island.

The night was black and no moon lit the sky. Hazel was asleep in her bunk. When we reached open water, the lightning flashes appeared high in the mountains of Haiti dead ahead of us. They did not let up and offered a near-constant illumination in the distance.

The longer I watched the lightning that we were sailing toward, the more frightened I became. But we sailed on and after a few worrisome hours, the lightning fizzled.

We pulled into port midmorning and the customs man boarded the boat. He spoke no English. The two official languages of Haiti are Creole and French. This could be interesting, I figured. We stared at each other for a bit, trying to figure out how to solve our little problem.

"Habla Espanol?" he said.

A wave of relief came over me. I'd taken a Spanish class before the trip, so maybe we could work this out after all.

"Un poquito," I told him.

The little bit of Spanish I'd learned was good enough, particularly after I poured him a drink. He cleared us all the way to Port-au-Prince, the capital.

When we stepped ashore, we were struck by the poverty and hunger. But the people were kind and gentle and ready to help a stranger in any way they could. If they had a garden, they'd offer you vegetables. If it was a fruit tree, they'd offer their fruit.

We'd brought with us a bag of old clothes and this seemed like a perfect place to pass them along. It made many hearts happy. People gathered around the boat and stood watching us for hours. They didn't beg, but it was clear they were hungry. Hazel started handing out rice and flour until we had little left ourselves. I had to tell her that if she kept it up we'd be as hungry as they were.

The following day we pushed on to Gonaives, one of the larger Haitian cities and as we pulled in, the open-air market was bustling. We strolled around it and perused all the strange island items that were for sale.

A food vendor was making sausage. As the lady worked on the open table, flies crawled all over the ground meat, which she packed into a pig gut, flies and all. She sold it as fast as she could make it.

Before we left the U.S., a sailing friend who owned a wholesale grocery business gave me a big bag of cigarettes and candy for the trip.

Back at the boat, where we were anchored off the beach, kids would swim out for the candy and we had a great time watching their reactions. Candy was a rare treat for them.

The cigarettes I saved for the customs men. On this trip, I developed a little ceremony when they boarded my boat. I'd give each a pack of cigarettes and a paper cup of booze. Most requested Scotch, but I had just one bottle. When it was gone, I refilled it with blended whiskey and they never knew the difference. They watched me pour from the bottle and then they'd sip from their cups and smack their lips, telling me how good it was.

From Gonaives we sailed to Ile de la Gonave and the following day into Port-Au-Prince. In the capital, we found a beautiful gated yacht club. Each boat had its own boat boy who cleaned and did any necessary work. I picked a young, friendly boy who called himself Che Che. He reported for work at sun-up and worked until sundown. I paid him five dollars per day. One of the boaters complained that I was overpaying him, that most boats were paying three dollars.

While Che Che took care of the boat, Hazel and I explored the city. One day I told our boat boy that I wanted him to take us around and show us all the sites. After a morning of sightseeing, we stopped for lunch in a nice restaurant and invited Che Che to join us.

He ordered the most expensive lunch on the menu, but after taking a few bites he said something to the waiter, who returned with a doggy bag. Che Che emptied his plate into the bag.

"This is for my family," he said.

It made me glad I was overpaying him.

At the marina, we struck up a friendship with a couple from Georgia, Howard and Hazel Hill. Howard had owned an air-conditioning business in Savannah. He'd retired and turned operations over to his son. His wife was a typical Southern belle, right down to the pleasing accent and the very proper manners.

Their boat was the Georgia Gypsy, and as fellow Americans in a foreign land, we got along well from the start. We discovered that they had a very similar trip planned. They'd been in town for more than a week when we got there and departed a few days before we did, but we'd see them again.

While in Port-au-Prince, I obtained clearance papers that allowed us to visit anywhere in the country. At each subsequent stop, the local official would board the Peace & Plenty and I'd flash the clearance documents.

"Good paper," the official would say, and we were free to go.

After a week in the capital, we started working our way around the long peninsula that juts out on the southwest corner of Haiti, and on to Jacmel, a very old coffee port and one of the most beautiful cities in Haiti.

As we pulled into the harbor at Jacmel, a man in a dugout canoe came out to meet us. He wore a somewhat official-looking cap and gestured for us to stop.

"This guy is going to try to rip me off," I told Hazel.

I allowed him to come aboard and he told me that he'd show me to my anchorage. As he stood with me in the cockpit, he said, "Full speed ahead," so I shot the fuel to my twenty-five horsepower diesel.

"Left full rudder," he said, and I gave it left full rudder.

Then he said," Stop all engines and drop the anchor."

I obliged.

"What do we do now?" I said.

"Well," he replied. "Most people give me ten dollars."

I was furious.

"Get the hell off my boat!"

And with that, he looked like he was going to cry. He begged me to let him be my boat boy. He said he'd go up on the mountain to fetch me water, because the water in town would make us sick.

I calmed down. I told him that he could start with the water and I would see how his work was. As it turned out, he was a good worker and he stayed with us until we departed Jacmel.

Leaving there, we continued east along the south coast stopping at any port that looked inviting. The people were wonderful to us and could not have been friendlier. For all their poverty and desperation, only once did we feel threatened.

It's common when visiting boats arrive in ports for Haitians to approach in canoes to check you out and see if you have anything to offer. Sometimes we did, as when we handed out the clothes and candy. But often, even if you have nothing to give, the Haitians in the canoes will linger, sometimes for hours.

One evening, as we sat at anchor, the canoes gathered. The sun sank low and all the canoes left, except for one boat carrying three young men. They didn't appear to be making any plans to leave, so I went below and came up with the sawed-off 12-gauge shotgun that I kept on the boat for protection. I sat on the deck and commenced wiping it down with a rag.

The three men began to talk to each other in low tones. I was getting impatient and a little worried, so I pumped a round into the chamber. This sound never fails to get a person's attention. I went back below and in a minute or so, they headed for shore.

To make sure, once it was dark, I got out my portable spotlight and played it around on the mountainside for a few minutes to let them know they couldn't sneak up in the dark.

It turned out to be a peaceful night at anchor.

The shotgun was always for show. I never had to use it, but it was a comfort to have it with me. There is no place in the world free from criminals and in a sailboat you are particularly vulnerable.

In the Bahamas, on another trip, I was awakened in the middle of the night by the sound of someone moving around on deck. I eased out of my bunk, pulled out that old shotgun and slid the hatch open. I trained the gun on the trespasser, who hadn't yet realized I was there.

"I'm going to kill you now, you sonofabitch," I said.

"I'm a policeman!" he yelled back.

"Policeman, my ass."

At that, he leapt off the boat and took off running. He'd been trying to steal a gas tank I had tied on deck. In his haste to leave, he'd left behind a bag of boat parts that he'd swiped off of the boat docked next to me. The next morning, I returned the boat parts to their owner, a friend named Bob who had received them by mail a day earlier.

I regret to this day that I didn't fire a shot in the air, alerting someone who might have caught the thief.

Dominican Republic

Leaving Haiti, we anchored off Isla Beata near the south coast of the Dominican Republic. Recent experiences had left me a little on edge, so I was less than hospitable when, upon our arrival, three men approached us in a boat, tied up alongside and attempted to come aboard.

In no uncertain terms, I made it clear that they could not set foot on deck. They hesitated, spoke a few quiet words to each other and disappeared.

I was beginning to get nervous, thinking maybe they had gone for reinforcements. And sure enough, before long, I saw their boat approaching again. I was ready for a confrontation but when they got close, I realized the three men had changed into the uniform of the Dominican navy.

I welcomed them aboard in my broken Spanish and pulled out an ID card that indicated I was retired from the U.S. Navy. We all had a drink and a laugh about the misunderstanding.

The island is a few minutes south of Cape Beata, which like most capes all over the world, funnels wind out to sea at an increased speed, making for rough waters. The anchorage there was unpleasant to say the least, and we moved on without lingering long.

Our next stop was to be Barahona, just to the north. We were going dead into the wind and my plan was to motor sail and make the best speed that I could. We pulled out after dark. But as we rounded the island, the wind hit us with its full force and the waters were treacherous. With each wave, the bow dipped into the sea and launched back out again.

The Peace & Plenty was riding like a bucking bronco.

After moving to the Keys, I'd spent long hours constructing a wind vane, which was the closest thing to autopilot I had in those days. The wind vane attached to a small underwater rudder, which in turn was linked to the steering wheel. You'd set the boat on a course and if the wind shifted a few degrees, the wind vane would correct the course and keep you going where you wanted to go. It saved me from many wet, windy and unpleasant hours on the deck.

The wind vane became the first casualty of our turbulent run to Barahona. When the boat came crashing down from one of the bigger waves, the underwater section of the wind vane snapped and sank to the bottom of the ocean.

I knew immediately what happened. I grabbed the wheel and called Hazel to come topside.

"Take the wheel," I told her.

The wind was blowing stronger than ever and the boat was rocking and rolling.

"I don't think I can," she said.

"You don't have a choice," I replied. "You have to take it and steer while I pull down the jib."

She grabbed the wheel and did a great job keeping the bow into the wind while all the sails flapped and water sprayed everywhere. We continued all night under violent conditions. A short time after the sun appeared, the wind eased and we pulled into Barahona at midmorning, battered and exhausted. Everything below deck was a mess, items big and small scattered about. It took days to get everything cleaned up and in order.

At the dock in Barahona, we found Howard Hill sitting aboard the Georgia Gypsy. Their run to Barahona had been just as unpleasant and upon completing it, Howard's wife, Hazel, had caught a plane and headed home. She'd had enough.

I asked my Hazel if she wanted to do the same. No, she said, but she admitted that the thought had crossed her mind during the last run. I was proud of her. She'd become a real blue-water sailor.

We stayed in Barahona for about a week, repairing some damage and allowing everything to dry out. It gave us time to explore and it was on this visit that we became acquainted with Dr. Luis Beltran Perez Espinosa, as well as his wife and daughter. Luis later became the ambassador of the division of American Affairs for the Dominican Secretary of State. It grew into a wonderful friendship and we'd see them many times over the years, visiting whenever we had the chance.

We departed Barahona in company with Georgia Gypsy and worked our way over to Santo Domingo. There we docked in the old colonial section of the city on the Ozama River, behind the home of Diego Columbus, the son of Christopher.

Zona Colonial has been restored to look like it would have in the 1500s, and walking its streets for the first time, it's as if history is rushing all around you. The cobblestone takes you past one building after another constructed in the 15th or 16th centuries. The only way to see it is on foot.

There is a Spanish fort that dates to the 1570s, and the first monastery in the New World. Down the hill from the residence of Diego Columbus is an imposing entryway built in 1571 as the main gate into the city. There is also the home of Hernan Cortes, conqueror of Mexico.

After a few days, Howard said so long and set his course for points south. Hazel and I stayed and enjoyed the endless sightseeing and I seized the opportunity to practice my Spanish. After a while, we moved over to Boca Chica Marina, the official yacht club of Santo Domingo, east of the city. It is a beautiful, well-equipped marina and had anything you wanted except hot water.

After a few days in the comfort of a full-service marina, we said goodbye to the big city and spent three days in La Romana before heading east across the Mona Passage, another stretch of water known for its rough seas and currents. Our trip across was no exception. Without a wind vane to help me steer, I had not been looking forward to it.

It was a rough and windy run and by the time we reached our anchorage on the west side of Isla Mona, I was more than ready to stop and get some sleep. But once there, we discovered that this was no place to rest.

The boat rocked and rolled and after a short time, Hazel became seasick trying to stay in her bunk. So I pulled the anchor and we were back under way, away from the Dominican.

Our time in Haiti and the Dominican Republic – a peculiar patch of earth shared by two nations at times very much alike and at other times very different – had been a real adventure for us and an eye-opening experience.

In Haiti, we didn't see a single outboard motor. All the boats, even those eighty-feet long, were operated by sail alone. It was like going back in time a hundred years. At night, we'd sit and listen to the beat of voodoo drums echoing down from the mountains. The people there had nothing and yet I was struck by their gentleness.

I made many journeys back to this country and found wonderful things each time.

As for the Dominican Republic, I fell in love with it on first sight. It is a beautiful, interesting country with a wonderful history, and the characters who live there ensure you will never leave without a story to tell. It's because of the Dominican people that I continued to speak Spanish and to study it and all things pertaining to their culture.

Puerto Rico

A few rough hours after departing Isla Mona, the water calmed and we pulled in to Mayaguez, Puerto Rico, after daylight. We cleared customs and collapsed into our bunks.

The anchorage there was also exposed to the wind and before long we moved south a few miles to Boqueron, a landlocked harbor with miles of broad, sandy beaches, a resort destination for Puerto Rican families.

As we pulled in to anchor, there sat Howard on the Georgia Gypsy. We passed the rest of the day drinking rum-and-Cokes and catching up on each other's adventures. Howard told us that years earlier he'd bought his boat from one of the owners of the Don Q rum company in Ponce, Puerto Rico, which was our next destination.

When we arrived there, we found dockage at a reasonable cost inside the town's beautiful yacht club. The former owners of Howard's boat came down to visit and they invited us all to a private New Year's Eve party at the yacht club the following day. It turned out to be a grand affair.

While swapping sea stories, I told of losing use of my wind vane en route to the Dominican mainland. A gentleman there said that he owned a shipping company in Ponce and promised that after the holiday he'd send the foreman of his machine shop down to the boat and that he'd build a replacement part at no cost. It felt more like Christmas than New Year's.

While waiting for my part to be finished, we toured Ponce, an old Spanish colonial town. In the middle of the town square, called Plaza Las Delicias, sits a vast 300-year-old cathedral, constructed of white stone and flanked by two square towers, each topped with a dome and a cross.

The town's art museum, the Museo de Arte de Ponce, is considered the finest in Puerto Rico.

After about a week of sightseeing, my new part was delivered and once more we headed east, grateful to again have some help with the steering. We worked our way down the south coast until we came to the Roosevelt Roads Naval Station, a U.S. base in the town of Ceiba. Howard kept going but Hazel and I stopped to get a little taste of the Navy culture we'd enjoyed for so long. Since I was retired Navy, we were able to use the base's marina. A bus came by every twenty minutes and made the rounds of the base. Hazel had a ball shopping in the Navy Exchange and the commissary, and we stocked up on provisions and liquor before departing for St. Thomas.

The Virgin Islands

On our arrival in St Thomas, in the U.S. Virgin Islands, it seemed we had returned to civilization. The harbor was packed with boats, coming and going. Two large cruise ships discharged passengers by the hundreds. Con artists hovered everywhere, trying to sell junk to the tourists. We were told to be careful on the street at night.

We didn't stay around very long, just long enough to say hello to a couple of old Navy friends who lived there and then we headed for the British Virgin Islands.

The BVIs were what I had imagined they would be. The sailing was superb, smooth water and fair breezes with each new island more beautiful than the last.

The only negative thing I found was the charter boats. Almost every night, we'd find a nice spot to anchor and after we'd settled in, we'd spot a giant charter boat headed in our direction. They must have been afraid of the dark because without fail they'd anchor as close to us as they could. More than once, I had to tell them to move away so our boats wouldn't bang together when the current shifted.

We worked our way over to Virgin Gorda, the jumping off point for a long haul to St. Martin. The wind was light as we left Virgin Gorda, so I put up the main sail and started the motor. We ran all afternoon and expected to arrive there around daylight the next morning. At around midnight, Hazel joined me on deck.

"You must be tired," she said. "Go lay down. I'll stand lookout while you get some sleep."

I offered no argument. I climbed down into the cabin, crawled into my bunk and drifted off. But I hadn't been asleep long when I heard Hazel calling to me.

"There's something ahead of us," she said.

"What is it?" I asked

She didn't know.

I came up to take a look and there dead ahead of us was the most gorgeous full moon, breaking the surface of the flat, calm sea. She had never seen such a sight and when I told her what it was, the two of us stood arm-in-arm watching it rise into the cloudless sky.

We arrived in Philipsburg on the Dutch side of St. Martin at daylight and dropped anchor. It was an open roadstead and the boat rolled at anchor, so after clearing customs we moved around the island to a landlocked lagoon called "The Pond" and settled in for a long stay. From that spot, it was a short dinghy ride to Marigot on the French side or Philipsburg on the Dutch side. We checked out both sides and it was no contest. The French side won hands down. It was almost like being back in Paris, the sidewalk cafes, the fabulous French cooking, not to mention the wine. What a wonderful place.

We hung around for days, lounging in the sun and taking in the towns. We were living the good life until, at last, the inevitable happened.

The good life started getting old.

Heading home

On any long trip, there comes a point when it's time to start heading back. Our return trip started off easy enough, with a great downwind sail back over to the Virgin Islands. As we approached Virgin Gorda, I started the engine is case we needed it. It was then that I noticed we had very little cooling water and the engine was running hot. I shut it down and we sailed on in to Road Town on the island of Tortola and found a diesel repair place with a dock.

The following day, the mechanic found a cracked head in the engine. The owner of the shop told me he'd have to order the new part from Miami. It would take about two weeks to arrive, but he promised us free dockage until then. So we settled in to enjoy life on Tortola.

It was an interesting little town, much to see during the day and plenty of nightlife after dark. But most evenings found us on the Peace & Plenty playing cards or backgammon for a penny a point. Booze was dirt cheap so we would pick up a bottle of Irish Cream to sip during the game. Most times I would lose interest and before we left there, I was in debt to my wife for hundreds of dollars.

While in Road Town, we most enjoyed the Saturday morning market. Native boats came from all directions, carrying vast varieties of local seafood. Women and children brought homegrown produce and meats. You had to get there early to get the good stuff.

Theirs is a beautiful harbor, semi-circular and surrounded by high green mountains. We passed many hours being entertained by the tourists coming and going in boats from a large charter company. They put on a great show coming into a dock or anchoring.

One person would go to the bow and most often they would start out with hand signals to each other. When one made a mistake, that person would accuse the other of relaying the wrong signal. Then they'd scream at each other as the boat crashed into the dock or overshot the anchorage.

The more people on board, the more confusion reigned.

When the engine part arrived from Miami, the boss assigned a mechanic to put the engine back together. Talk about slow. I thought he might fall asleep in the middle of rebuilding the engine. I was growing frustrated and I went to the boss.

I told him I could not afford this very slow mechanic, but the boss assured me that his man was the best around and that I was not being charged by the hour.

Though it took a while, the mechanic did an outstanding job, and the price was very fair.

We proceeded to St. Thomas and as we entered the harbor of Charlotte Amalie there sat the Georgia Gypsy swinging on its anchor. Once we anchored, Howard came over in his dinghy for a visit.

He had made it to Trinidad after picking up a friend to help with the boat in his wife's absence. He told us that on their arrival it was Carnival and his friend made the mistake of wandering off alone.

When he returned to the boat in the wee hours, he was nude. He had been rolled, robbed of everything he had on him, including his clothes.

I'm not sure how he managed to negotiate the city streets to get back to the boat. At that time of the morning, I guess no one paid any attention.

After catching up on sea stories, I put steaks on the grill. Then with full bellies, we settled down to some serious drinking and storytelling. When Hazel excused herself and went below to her bunk, Howard and I decided that we needed to go to the marina and see what was going on at the bar.

As we pulled into the dock, I attempted to step out of the dinghy but somehow managed to capsize the little boat, motor and all. We had our cocktail glasses so we began bailing out the boat with our glasses.

A woman stopped and asked if we were OK. We told her that, yes, we were fine. We just had to finish bailing out the boat.

What a night that was.

We didn't run into Howard again on that trip, but we never lost touch with him and he visited us once in the Keys.

Years later, while driving to Maryland, I decided to return the favor and drop in on Howard and Hazel at their home outside Savannah. Their house was a typical Southern mansion set at the end of a long driveway lined on each side with magnolia trees. Columns stretched across the front of the house.

A maid answered when I rang the doorbell, and I asked to see Howard and Hazel.

"Are you family?" the maid asked.

"No," I said, "but a very close friend."

She asked me to wait and disappeared into the house. After a moment, Hazel came to the door and invited me in. She had bad news. Howard had been diagnosed with cancer. He had only months to live. To make things worse, a stroke had left him incapacitated.

Hazel showed me to his bedroom and I found him there lying on the bed, wearing only a diaper, with tears pouring down his face. But his eyes lit up when I walked in. He recognized me and managed a smile. He could no longer form words, but the sounds he made told me he was happy to see me.

I sat with him and held his hand. There wasn't much to say and after a while, I left. It was the last time I'd see my old sailing buddy.

Within days, we made our way back to Roosevelt Roads in Puerto Rico. We'd been gone for five months and Hazel was ready to be home. I told her we could find her a flight from Puerto Rico, but she would not leave me to travel back alone. I found a phone and called two friends from the Keys to join me for the last leg of the journey. They jumped at the opportunity.

I rented a car and drove Hazel to the airport in San Juan, picking up Lloyd Knouse and Ray Sulliven the same day.

The next day, again with access to all the shops on the base, we provisioned the boat for the trip back. I also took them to the base liquor store and when they saw the prices they went crazy and almost bought out the store. We had a well-oiled crew all the way home.

With the wind behind us, we set a course for the north coast of Puerto Rico, stopped for the night at the very small harbor of Arecibo, and got underway early the next morning for the Dominican Republic.

We had a wonderful, exciting day crossing the Mona Passage. It was the time for migration of the humpback whales, and we had a free show the entire day.

The weather was perfect with a downwind sail and we saw hundreds of whales broaching. These huge animals would lift themselves out of the water, and then come crashing back in. Many of them were larger than our boat and only yards away from us, but at no time did we feel fear.

We sailed on through the night, arriving the next morning at Puerto Santa Barbara in the Dominican. After clearing customs, we dropped sixty-five cents apiece and enjoyed a breakfast of bacon and eggs and then passed the day strolling around town and sitting under an umbrella at an outdoor cafe near the dock, sipping wonderful Dominican beer.

The following day, we had a twenty-four-hour run to our next port, Puerto Plata. This is one of the major cities on the north coast and at that time the only official port of entry. It's a typical Spanish colonial town with large plaza, complete with bandstand and concerts on the weekends. We lingered for a few days, finding another umbrella at another café and plenty more beers.

Ten miles east is the town of Sousa, with a small harbor on the west side of Cape Macoris and a great anchorage on a long sandy beach.

The town is a Jewish resettlement community, started in 1940 as a means of saving thousands of Jews fleeing Hitler's Germany. They were allowed to settle there and in time built a thriving dairy industry and a model town with good roads, an electrical plant and many businesses.

Since their arrival, the Jewish inhabitants have blended well into their adopted country, some taking Spanish names, but they worship in the same small synagogue that was built in those early days when the world had gone mad.

Puerto Plata, however, is well known as the home of Brugal Rum and it was almost my downfall.

We'd planned to leave in the afternoon in order to arrive at our next port, Cap Haitien, during daylight hours the following day. So that morning, we took one more trip into town.

One of the few places we hadn't visited was the rum plant. They greeted us like family, gave us each a paper cup, pointed to a faucet with a never-ending supply of rum and insisted that we could drink all we wanted.

One cup called for a second and a second for a third and so on. We staggered out in midafternoon and somehow found the marina. Lloyd pointed out some bad-looking clouds rolling in.

"Hell with them," I said, full of rum-powered disregard.

We climbed aboard and no sooner than we'd made it out to sea, a thunderstorm hit and it felt like the end of the world was upon us.

Lloyd was at the wheel and I was struggling with the sails. His experience was with power boats, and he put all his strength into trying to keep us on course. In doing so, he snapped one of the cable fittings and lost all steering.

I dug out the emergency tiller and rigged it up. We sailed all the way to Cap Haitien by tiller. On arriving, I told them to go and see the Citadel, the big attraction we had been planning to visit, and I spent the day repairing the boat.

God punishes those who are stupid.

We left the following day. But I later made many trips back to this port and got to know it well. Cap Haitien is a charming place with first-class hotels and fine dining in the French tradition. It is far more enjoyable, cleaner and less crowded than Port-au-Prince.

The Citadel is the mountain fortress of Henri Christophe, leader of the Haitian slave rebellion and later the self-proclaimed king. The

Citadel will overwhelm you. It sits atop a mountain nearly 3,000 feet above sea level. Construction took thirty years.

In the reefs to the east of the port in Cap Haitien is the final resting place of the Santa Maria, the flagship of Columbus' voyage of discovery. Some of my diving friends took part in a dive sponsored by the inventor and explorer Ed Link and recovered the anchor of the Santa Maria, along with some other artifacts, which today are on display in a museum in Port-au-Prince.

Upon checking into port at Cap Haitien, you are required to turn in any firearms, so I handed over my old sawed-off 12 gauge. When we were ready to leave, I requested my gun and the official went to retrieve it. He returned with a beautiful 30-06 hunting rifle and as he went to hand it to me, I instinctively responded that it was not my gun. I'd passed up a good deal. He turned around and returned with my rusty old shotgun.

Leaving Cap Haitien, we set a course for Great Inagua in the Bahamas. It would be another long run. One of the problems we encountered was Sully. He was getting up in years. I'm not sure how old he was and I'm not convinced he knew himself. Standing watch at night in the cool wind caused him a lot of joint pain, so we made a deal that Lloyd and I would stand watch at night if Sully did all the cooking.

He was very happy with that arrangement and he sat in the cabin most nights drinking from the vast supply of booze he'd bought in Puerto Rico.

Our stove at that time was fueled by kerosene and to light it you had to fill a priming cup with alcohol and heat the burner prior to turning on the kerosene. It was a complicated process for a sober person and, during this run, Sully was something less than sober. After dinner, he failed to completely turn off one of the knobs, which allowed kerosene to drip all night into the pan below the burners.

At daylight, fifty miles out to sea, Sully began the process of starting the stove to get the morning coffee ready. The flames came fast. I was at the wheel when suddenly it looked like the entire boat was on fire. I raced to grab a fire extinguisher from a cockpit locker and let loose on the stove, killing the fire before serious damage could be done. It was a close call. We kept an eye on Sully after that, but thankfully our trip was winding down.

Before daylight the next day, we picked up the lighthouse at Great Inagua and sailed into the small marina at Mathew Town. Morton Salt has a giant operation there. They harvest over a million tons of salt per year from the island's extensive salt pan.

The town is also the home of Inagua National Park, a sanctuary for the world's largest breeding population of the West Indian flamingo. More than 50,000 of them roam the area. My crew spent the day touring the park while I stayed on the boat, catching up on repairs.

From there, we worked our way north to Great Exuma Island, spent the night in George Town and then headed up Exuma Sound. That morning, weather reports indicated a violent storm on the way so we diverted our course to Hatchet Bay, a landlocked hurricane hole with plenty of protection.

We sailed through some heavy seas to get there and it was a wet ride but we made it into the bay and the dockmaster, a friend of mine, had saved a spot for us. We made it just in time. It turned out to be a hell of a storm and we were fortunate not to be caught in it.

The next day dawned to beautiful weather, but I discovered that a port had leaked in the closet and soaked everything inside. Most of it was clothes Hazel had left aboard, so I dug out all of her things and hung them on the deck to dry – bras, panties and all. Without a female on board, we got quite a few remarks.

On the third day, we departed Hatchet Bay for Nassau and spent a night there before brief stops at Chub Cay and Bimini, where we waited for good weather to cross the Gulf Stream back to Florida. Once nature obliged, we had a nice, smooth run to the Keys.

When we approached Snake Creek, we hung the flags of all the countries the Peace & Plenty had visited on the trip and as we eased down the canal, Hazel and all our neighbors gathered on the dock to welcome us home.

I'd been away six months and enjoyed every day of it. So ended the first Caribbean trip of the Peace & Plenty. It would not be the last.

In the coming decades, Hazel and I spent at least two or three months in the Bahamas or the Caribbean every year. The experiences we had and the friendships we made lasted far longer.

LONG-HAIRED BILLY

The phone rang inside our home in the Florida Keys and the moment I answered it I knew that I should not have. My next instinct was to hang up the phone, but there was a ghost on the line and curiosity got the better of me.

The voice on the other end was one from my past, an old Navy shipmate by the name of Billy Steele. We chatted for a few minutes, about old times, before the true motivation behind the call revealed itself. Billy needed a favor.

This is why I should have hung up the phone.

Billy was an acquaintance from my time as an instructor at the Explosive Ordnance Disposal school in Indian Head. He was one of several diving instructors, but I remember him most as an outdoorsman, always out in the woods hunting whatever game was in season or out on the water with a fishing rod in hand.

Billy was a good guy, but he wasn't exactly a top-notch Navy man. That's why it was so surprising when we found out those years ago that he had suddenly and without explanation, at least to the rest of us, been commissioned as an officer. We figured the Navy must have mixed up his paperwork with some other sailor, someone a little more squared away. He was not officer material.

For a while, all was well. But then it wasn't. An EOD demonstration for a group of visiting VIPs went horribly, fatally wrong when some explosives detonated prematurely. Billy survived without being badly injured, but he left the Navy and moved down to Florida, to the swampland along the Crystal River. That's where he was when he reached into the past and dialed my number.

I hadn't heard his name or thought of him in years, but here he was telling me about this job he had for me, delivering a boat from Puerto Rico back to Florida.

He needed me because the boat's insurance required that its operator have a captain's license. I had it, he did not. He asked me to go with him, promising we'd split the take. An easy job, he assured me, because the boat was in great condition.

The money was right and if what Billy told me was accurate, it sounded too good to be true. Well, you know what they say about things that are too good to be true.

Anyway, he had talked me into it. My own boat, the Peace & Plenty, was loaded up and ready for a trip down south that I'd been planning. But my trip would have to be postponed.

A thirty-eight-foot sailboat waited for us at a marina in Fajardo, on the east coast of Puerto Rico. Hazel dropped me at the airport in Miami and as she drove off she was mumbling something about how I should take care of myself because Billy sure wouldn't. Yeah, she knew Billy, too.

I'd arranged to meet him at the airport and when he walked up I couldn't believe my eyes. Billy was a walking head of hair. All you could see were his eyes peeking out between the mop on his head and a shaggy beard.

"Billy, you look like a dope-headed hippie," I told him. "What rock did you crawl out from under?"

He came back with some nonsense about trying to catch up on living after all those years in the Navy. This, I figured, would be an interesting trip.

He'd brought his son Joe with him to help stand watch and so the three of us boarded a plane for Puerto Rico. After arriving, we rented a car and headed straight for the marina to find the boat, which Billy at this point warned me had been sitting there idle for some time. It was my first clue that Billy's assessment of the boat had been somewhat less than forthcoming.

When we opened the hatch, I think even Billy wanted to turn around and go home. Inside the cabin, which had been locked up in the tropic heat with no ventilation, cockroaches scurried in every direction, picking at scraps of food left lying about. There were thousands of them, a full-blown cockroach army.

We closed the hatch and drove straight to the nearest store, where we bought not a can but an entire case of roach spray. We went right to work, spraying and roach bombing the boat for days, staying at a hotel because the cabin was not habitable.

After a few days, we bested the cockroaches, so we moved onto the boat. Our biological assault, however, had left its mark and from that point on the drinking water aboard the boat tasted the way cockroach spray smells. It wasn't long before I swore off the water altogether and replaced it with stronger drink.

Examining the engine, I was surprised. The 25-horsepower Volvo was in decent shape. If we were lucky, it might last until we got back to Florida. But to be safe, I told them, we should only use it for entering and leaving port. The sails were in rough shape, old and rotting, but they would have to do. Within a few days, we were on our way.

The first day's sail took us around the north side of Puerto Rico to San Juan, and the following morning we were under way at daylight, heading to the west end of the island, where we planned to anchor for the night before crossing the Mona Passage to the Dominican Republic.

Sailing along next day, the northeast trade wind continued to increase, as it always does in that part of the world, and as we finished lunch we heard a frightening sound.

The main sail ripped from one end to the other. Not good.

We were coming up on Arecibo, on the northern midwest coast of Puerto Rico. We'd have to stop there and figure our next move. The port was barely a port at all, very small, protected from the trade winds but vulnerable to anything stronger.

The weather was stable, though, and was expected to be so for the next few days, so in we went. We started the engine to pull us into port but after a few minutes we heard a loud bang and the engine went silent. Powered by what remaining sails we had left, we managed to ease in and drop anchor.

I inspected the engine and found that we'd broken a valve, which meant a big repair job. Even if we could find someone in the area to overhaul the engine, we'd need to get the spare parts from San Juan. And we'd have to clear it with the boat's owner. All of this would take time, and we had no protection in the small harbor if the weather turned bad. We could not stay. I came up with a plan.

I'd spent a lot of time on the south coast of the Dominican Republic and knew of a small boatyard, run by an American, in the little town of La Romana. It would be a downwind sail all the way.

The boat yard was inside the mouth of the Rio Salado River. There was always plenty of boat traffic there, so it would be no problem to get a tow into the yard. We climbed into our bunks for a good night's sleep in preparation for the long haul awaiting us.

In the early hours, we were awakened by a group of men climbing aboard our boat. They were DEA agents, the Drug Enforcement Agency, and they suspected we were running narcotics. When they saw Billy, with his long hair and beard, they must have thought they'd hit the jackpot.

The agents spent hours pillaging the boat, searching every inch, before around noon, dejected, they gave up. We got the hell out of there.

We had no engine and no main sail, just the jib and the very small mizzen to push us along. It would be a night crossing of the Mona

Passage and if the trade winds held, I estimated we would arrive at La Romana during daylight hours.

We had only a compass to guide us and had to estimate the power of the current as well as our own speed to figure our progress.

Two hours on and four hours off, we took turns standing watch and hand steering the boat because we had no electricity and no autopilot. I stood the midnight-to-2 a.m. watch before Billy relieved me. I warned him to keep a sharp eye out for trouble. Then I headed into the cabin to get some sleep.

It was almost 4 a.m. when he shook me awake and told me to come topside.

"Look straight ahead and tell me what you see," he said.

I squinted into the darkness and as my eyes acclimated I could begin to make out white water in the distance and beyond it sheer white cliffs that looked at least fifty feet high. If we continued on this course, we'd sail straight into the raging surf that was breaking against the vertical cliffs. Even if we escaped with our lives, we'd be stranded miles from civilization in one of the most remote parts of the Dominican.

It looked bleak, but Mother Nature stepped in. The wind shifted and we moved to a more southerly course, narrowly avoiding disaster. When daylight arrived, we discovered how far off course we'd strayed. I'd been very wrong in my estimation of the speed of the currents and the slow speed of our disabled boat.

We limped into La Romana in late afternoon, got a tow up the river into the boat yard, where the following day, Billy began working out the details of the engine overhaul. He contacted the boat's owner and got the go-ahead. A new main sail was ordered and they worked up a list of other equipment that would be needed. Billy would fly back to the States and return with the new equipment.

It was all more than I'd bargained for. To get this boat ready to complete its journey was going to take quite a while, and I was itching to get home and climb onto my own boat for the trip I'd postponed to join in this circus with Billy.

He was sympathetic and told me that he'd find someone to take my place. When he left for the States, I'd be going with him, and going home.

After we finished compiling a list of everything he needed to bring back with him, I told him we needed to have a serious talk. I explained that I knew the Dominican Republic very well, that I loved the country and its people, and that I'd gotten to know the customs and immigration people very well. He was going to have to deal with them to bring back all this equipment.

"If there's one thing they all have in common," I told Billy, "it's their dislike of hippies. If you don't get a shave and a haircut, you're going to have problems with them when you try to get back into the country."

"OK, I'll think about it," was all he said.

That night we went into town, had a few drinks and tried out some of the local seafood, which we enjoyed very much. But the next day, Billy had big problems.

In Mexico, they call it "Montezuma's Revenge." I don't know if they have a name for it in the Dominican, but Billy was in rough shape. He wasn't good for much of anything. What little time he wasn't in the head, he was flat on his back in the bunk.

The following morning at breakfast, Billy managed only to drink a cup of coffee. We'd rented a car to drive to the airport in Santo Domingo for the flight home. I took the wheel so Billy could sprawl out in the back seat. The route to the airport was an easy one, a good main highway all the way. About halfway there, Billy got frantic.

"Stop the car! Stop the car! Stop the goddamn car!" he screamed.

I slammed the brakes and skidded to a stop on the side of the road. The door flung open and Billy jumped out, dropped his pants and did some business right there in the middle of bumper-to-bumper traffic in both directions. The image is seared into my memory.

We made it to the airport and went inside to purchase our tickets, whereupon Billy discovered that he'd left his credit card on the boat.

"I know just where I left it," he said, which did us no good at all.

I bought both tickets, telling him that if I didn't get my money back, I'd be coming to the swamp to take it out of his hide. He promised to repay me.

In Miami, we went our separate ways. I went home and then on my sailing trip. By the time I'd returned to Islamorada, it had been months since I'd heard from Billy. Then one day, he showed up unannounced in my driveway, still shaggy as hell, presented me with the money he owed and regaled me with the story of his further adventures with the sailboat.

He had, as I warned him, run into trouble attempting to go through customs in the Dominican. The agents confiscated all his new equipment and hassled him for days before relenting and allowing him to proceed to the boat, get it fixed and complete his journey.

"Billy, do you remember the conversation we had on the boat?"

"Yes, I remember," he said.

"Then I don't feel a lot of sorrow for you."

About a year later, his wife called to tell me Billy had died from stomach cancer. She described how much he had suffered. He'd gotten sick shortly after seeing me for the last time.

Thinking back on how sick he had been during our time in La Romana, I wondered if that might have been the beginning of the end. At any rate, he had delivered the boat to its owner, paid off his debts and put his affairs in order before leaving this world.

I hope he ended up in his happy hunting ground. If so, I am sure he is content.

WAYWARD SAILORS

The sea is an unpredictable place and a sailboat can give you fits every chance it gets.

I had my share of trying moments and misfortune over the years, but every so often out on the water you run into folks who are so unqualified to be piloting a ship that it makes your little mishaps pale in comparison. It puts things in perspective and if nothing else, it makes you glad you are not them.

In the 1970s, Hazel and I were attempting to cross the Gulf Stream on our way to Bimini when we ran into a violent storm that blew us off course. During these early days, we often cruised with nothing more than a compass for navigation. Sometimes, I'd lose my bearings.

I'd expected to come into view of Bimini about 4 a.m., but daylight came and still I saw no land. I was relieved when I spotted a sailboat in the distance, and I steered the Peace & Plenty in its direction, hoping to get a fix on where we were and how far from Bimini we'd strayed.

As I pulled up alongside, I saw two long-haired types sitting in the cockpit smoking funny cigarettes. My optimism faded.

"Can you tell me where Bimini is located?" I asked.

"No, man," one responded. "We've been looking for it for three days."

The stoned sailors were going to be of no help, so I bid them good luck and sailed off. A short time later, a power boat came along and I called to them on the radio. I asked for a position, they provided it and we proceeded on to Bimini.

We stayed there for three days, enjoying ourselves. The pot smokers never did show up.

On another trip, I was anchored in a favorite spot at Landrail Point on Crooked Island in the Bahamas with Hal Smithers, a lawyer friend of mine who had sailed over with me. We'd finished dinner and were sitting around sipping on a few rum-and-Cokes when we heard the VHF radio come to life.

"Mayday, Mayday, Mayday!" a voice called out. "We are lost, we are running out of food and water, and we need help."

I answered the call and a man explained that there were three people aboard the boat. They'd left Tortola in the British Virgin Islands two weeks earlier and they had not a clue where they were. I told him that we were anchored near the Bird Rock Lighthouse, which had a twenty-five-mile range, and we were talking on a VHF radio, which also had a twenty-five-mile range.

"Get on deck," I told him, "and look for the light."

Ten minutes passed before we heard the voice again.

"We see it, we see it!"

I told them to come on in toward the west side of the light and they'd see our boat.

"Anchor near us," I said, "and we'll see you in the morning."

When the sun rose, we awoke to see them putting one man ashore. It turned out the boat belonged to a couple in their sixties who had moved to Florida from up north. They'd recently married and, though neither of them had much experience on the water, they'd decided to buy a sailboat.

The couple had found this particular boat for sale in Tortola, bought it and then advertised for a crew who could bring them back to

Florida. The man who answered the ad was an instructor in navigation for the Power Squadron, a civilian group focused on boating safety, somewhere up north and when he reported aboard, he brought his sextant and all his navigation tables.

They set a course for Florida and within a week he was lost and in such a panic that he could not obtain a position. When the boat made it to Crooked Island, the owners kicked their man off the boat and told him they never wanted to see him again.

But they didn't know what to do next.

I advised them to hire a local man, Willie Gibson, to captain the boat and take them to the Keys. Willie had been making a living on boats all his life, and he was more than qualified.

We were leaving that day to go over to George Town to see the annual Out Island Regatta, one of the biggest events in the Bahamas. After a few days, the couple showed up in George Town with Willie at the helm. They stayed only two days and backing out of the slip at the marina, they discovered that the transmission had gone out. The owner of the boat came over and again asked my advice.

I told him to get on a plane, go home and let Willie take care of the problem. He could sail their boat back to the Keys. The man would not hear of it. He insisted on staying aboard to look after his boat. I shrugged and wished him a good trip home.

Later in the day, he hired a boat to tow them out to open water where they could sail by the wind. Off they went.

Months later, I ran into the woman in Islamorada. We recognized each other, and after some small talk, I asked about their trip home. All pleasantness disappeared from her face. It was a tale of horror, she said.

With no motor, the boat was at the mercy of the wind. And as luck would have it, there was not much wind, leaving them to float in the open water making no progress. When the wind did come, she said, it came hard and made for rough seas.

Either way, it was miserable.

It took the newlyweds a month to travel from the Bahamas to the Keys and by the time they'd arrived, she and her husband could no longer stand the sight of each other.

They sold the boat and got a divorce.

CANCER

In 1994, Hazel's health began to slip away from her and the diagnosis was Type II diabetes. In the beginning, we hardly noticed. She was very active. We traveled and did all the things we loved to do.

But gradually, a little more each day, her energy and vitality were draining from her. We blamed the diabetes and thought maybe she could get it under control, get back to her old self. She didn't want to slow down, and I hoped she wouldn't. But she did. Much as we wished it was not the case, it was unavoidable.

She decided one day the following spring that a trip to Maryland was in order. She wanted to see her daughters, and so we made the plans and off we went, driving in our new conversion van that was a house on wheels. The trip passes through Orlando and Hazel wanted to stop at Disney World. I agreed, on the condition that she let me rent a wheelchair for her. Walking for any length of time was exhausting. She swallowed her pride and allowed it.

We booked a room at one of the nicer hotels inside the resort and, despite the wheelchair, she was laughing and smiling and joking. We took in several shows, toured the park and then were on our way north again.

In Maryland, we had a great visit, catching up with our daughters and our grandchildren and hearing all the latest updates in their lives. It was one of the most enjoyable trips we'd taken in some time. I thought Hazel seemed energized and happy. But the girls must have sensed that all was not well.

Before long, they called and said they were planning a trip to visit us in the Keys. On the phone with Hazel, they asked her to make an appointment at a local photography studio to have pictures taken, the mother and her three daughters.

When she hung up the phone, Hazel looked at me and laughed.

"They must think I'm going to die," she said. "And they want to take pictures before it happens."

It was only a few weeks after their visit that Hazel grew much weaker and we made an appointment with a new doctor. She'd seen dozens of doctors in the preceding months and all of them blamed the diabetes. This time it was different.

Ovarian cancer, one of the most vicious forms of the disease.

Listening to the doctor deliver the diagnosis felt like a knife going through my chest. I was devastated. Weak as she was, Hazel was the strong one. I wanted to comfort her, but I found her assuring me. That's how she was. When anything bad happened in our lives, she was unshakeable. She was going to beat cancer. Damn the odds.

The doctor told us that she needed surgery. It was scheduled for two days later at Fishermen's Community Hospital in Marathon, and he said that after the surgery and a heavy dose of chemotherapy, she had a fair chance of survival.

We took that sliver of hope and clung to it.

Sandie and Andie flew down from Maryland. Our youngest daughter, Terri, lived in the Keys and all of them joined us at the hospital. I'll never forget sitting alone with Hazel in her room before the surgery. She patted her pillow and asked me to lie down beside her. I tried to ease her mind. I told her that we'd be sharing a pillow for many more years. I tried hard to believe it myself. As always, she was more worried about my own well-being than her own.

They wheeled her into the operating room, and I walked with the girls to the hospital chapel. We spent the afternoon sitting there in silence, asking God to protect her.

On that day, he did.

She made it through the operation and by the next morning she insisted she was fine, telling us all how much she loved us and pleading with us not to worry over her. Over the next week or so, she appeared more and more refreshed. The improvement was undeniable and when the doctors said she could go home, I had her back in our house by the end of the day. The relief I felt to see her resting in our own bed was immeasurable.

It was also temporary.

That night, she woke me from my sleep. She was in terrible pain. I hustled her to the car and raced to the emergency room. The cancer was spreading. She needed another operation immediately.

The happiness of her homecoming had been replaced by another dose of terror, and it happened so quickly it was beyond my comprehension. It tore at my heart to see her wheeled away for the first surgery and it was happening again.

The second operation lasted much longer. Once again, I prayed, but I admit my faith wavered. I questioned God. How could he let this happen to Hazel? Why give us hope and take it away?

She pulled through the operation, but with a little less pep this time. Morphine dripped into her veins as she lay in the hospital bed. When the pain grew unbearable, she'd push a button at her bedside for a heavier dose. I cornered her doctors every chance I got and pestered them with questions. All of them boiled down to one thing: "What are her chances?"

I wanted a straight answer. I never got it. Instead, it was always the same spiel about how far the medical field had advanced in treating cancer and how once she was strong enough, they'd start chemotherapy and things would get better.

What they wouldn't tell me was the truth: My wife of thirty-seven years was dying.

I retired each night, frustrated and helpless, to the small bed in our van, which I kept parked outside the hospital so I would always be close to her. I tried not to envision my life without her, because when I did, I saw nothing left.

Days later, she was transferred to Baptist Hospital in Miami. We were told that this hospital was better equipped to deal with Hazel's case, but I believe that they didn't want her death on their hands.

The doctors at Baptist Hospital leveled with us right away. It was almost hopeless, they said. Time was running out, but they would make her as comfortable as possible.

The reality of it was starting to hit Hazel. She was only sixty-eight years old. Rather than lashing out at fate, she lashed out at the hospital room. It was too small, she said. She wanted a bigger room.

It was small, but it was a fine room, especially by hospital standards, with its mahogany trim and furnishings.

"This is a beautiful room," I told her. "It looks like a ship's cabin."

"I knew you were going to say that," she replied.

The following day, she asked me to go to the store and bring back a pen and a notepad. She wanted me to write down all the different phases of her illness and all the different doctors she saw, when and where it all happened. She wanted a record of everything. I am not entirely sure why, but we got it down. Every bit of it.

At the end of the day, I kissed her goodnight. As I started to leave, I heard her call to me.

"I don't want you coming in here too early tomorrow," she said, and I promised her I wouldn't.

They were the last words she ever said to me. The phone rang at 2 a.m. She was gone.

The funeral was going to be in Maryland, where she would be buried beside her mother. I decided to drive up in the van. I needed a couple days of peace and quiet to wrap my mind around everything that had happened. Less than two months had passed since the discovery of the cancer. It was all too fast.

About halfway to Maryland, I stopped for the night and crawled into the bunk in the back of the vehicle. I hadn't been asleep long when something roused me awake. I opened my eyes and saw Hazel sitting on the edge of the bed.

"I just wanted to check on you before I left," she said. "I had to know that you were all right."

I told her not to worry, that I would be fine. Then she disappeared.

It was as real as anything I have ever experienced. She was there, she was absolutely there, and I will be sure of that fact as long as I live.

We buried Hazel on a sunny July day, and as we sat in those metal folding chairs at the gravesite, listening to the preacher speak words of comfort, a butterfly flitted around her casket. For a long time, I felt like I had died, too.

I sold the house in the Keys. Too many rooms, too many memories. But I found my peace aboard the Peace & Plenty. Maybe it was my military training, where it was instilled in me to pick myself up and keep going. Maybe it was the sea. But I kept going. I kept sailing, kept searching, and little by little I found myself again.

Still, whenever my mind wanders back over the years, it always settles on Hazel. She was my inspiration, my role model, always there to advise me and keep me out of trouble. She was the love of my life. And the life we shared for thirty-seven years was one of such happiness that it has sustained me in the years without her.

When we walked down the street, men looked at me with envy because of the beautiful woman on my arm. She was more beautiful than they knew.

She will always be by my side.

CUBA

I'd spent decades crisscrossing the Caribbean aboard the Peace & Plenty, checking out the big islands and the small ones, from the Bahamas on down. But I couldn't shake the feeling that there was one big island that I'd ignored. It wasn't without reason, but with Hazel gone, I wasn't feeling particularly cautious. I had no one to answer to. I was finally going to go.

Cuba.

I'm well aware of the history between Cuba and the United States. It would perhaps be more accurate to say the history between Fidel Castro's regime and the United States government. Living in South Florida, there is no shortage of Cubans, courageous folks who risked their lives for a chance at freedom on American shores. Once here, they shared their rich culture.

A good friend volunteered to joined me. At his request, I'll call him "Jack," to protect his identity. I guess Jack didn't want me to go alone. There was a strict economic embargo in place, which meant that we'd be committing a crime to spend money there, so we provisioned the boat with all we figured to need and made plans to be self-sustaining.

We routed our trip through the Bahamas, cruising first to George Town and on through Hog Cay Cut, a very shallow passage and no

185

place for a beginner. On the south side of the cut, we headed for the Jumentos, a chain of cays stretching ninety miles along the southeast corner of Grand Bahama Bank. It offers little in the way of shelter, and the Bahamas Guide warns that "in winter, this can be a stormy area." It was January.

The seas were rough but we made it down to Ragged Island, the last in this group, without incident and anchored at a settlement called Duncan Town, with a population of fewer than a hundred people. You know you're in Duncan Town when you see a massive DC-3 airliner that looks as if it crash-landed atop a bar called Percy's Eagle's Nest.

The DC-3 did crash, some time ago, into nearby waters. But it was raised and plopped down on top of the bar, where it became a prime tourist attraction. A gangplank leads from the bar into the plane, and you can bring your drink and enjoy the day from this most peculiar perch.

After a day in Duncan Town, we set a course for Bahia Naranjo, an inlet on the eastern end of Cuba's north coast. The weather was beautiful during the sail, so we put out a fishing line and around noon hooked a massive wahoo. We figured he weighed about seventy pounds and we spent the rest of the day dressing him out and cleaning up the mess we'd made in the process. The meat from that fish filled our small refrigerator and then some.

We sailed all night and after daylight, we neared the entrance to Puerta de Vita Marina. I called on the VHF radio and received a friendly welcome and instructions on where to tie up once inside.

Six Cuban officials boarded the Peace & Plenty once we'd made the dock and they began their very detailed check-in procedure. It took about four hours, a bit of paperwork and some persuasion to complete. I had a short-wave receiver that I used to get weather updates, but the dockmaster was adamant that it was also a transmitter, which would have been prohibited. For hours, I pleaded my case and he remained unconvinced.

He called in someone more acquainted with radios and asked him to inspect it. His expert declared that I was correct.

Of course, we did have a transmitting device, a little Magellan satellite communicator. It had a small keyboard that could be operated with a single finger, but it was enough to send email and receive them. Jack's wife had asked him to send dispatches describing our great adventure. But Jack told her that wasn't going to happen. He was no Ernest Hemingway, he said, but even Hemingway had no use for one-finger typing. Anyway, the Cuban officials never found the Magellan. Had they, it surely would have disappeared.

Toward the end of the inspection, the dockmaster disappeared with our passports. He returned with them an hour later and told us we were free to go ashore.

Our first order of business was making sure the fish didn't go to waste and we were able to pass some off to foreign boaters in the marina. I offered some to local Cubans, but was surprised at the response. First, they looked around as if to see if they were being watched. They thought it over, but declined. They were scared. The fish in Cuban waters belonged to Castro's government, and they wouldn't risk being caught.

Cuba's poverty was astounding. Even if we'd wanted to buy groceries there, we could not have. Stores distributed bread, rice, beans and other items in exchange for ration cards. One of the customs men told me he could only get six small rolls each week, but that he'd eat them all in one sitting. It had to be awful, I figured, and I asked him what he thought about Fidel Castro.

He commenced telling me what a wonderful man Castro was and how he was a great and powerful leader. I asked how he could feel that way since he'd just finished telling me he could not get enough to eat.

"Before Fidel, I was nobody," the customs man said. "Now, I am someone. I'm as good as anyone on the street."

I looked around and saw that most of the Cubans wore nothing more than rags for clothes, but as I traveled more throughout the country, I came to know that this customs man was not alone. Most of the Cubans loved Fidel. It was at odds with everything I believed of the place, my impression shaped by images of Cubans floating toward Florida on whatever partially seaworthy vessel they could piece together.

On the island, transportation consisted mostly of horse-drawn wagons and carts. Hitchhiking was the preferred method of travel and roads were almost nonexistent, except around the large tourist hotels.

After a few days of sightseeing, we checked out of the marina, which only required ten minutes and one man. We then began the long run back through the Bahamas and on to Florida.

But I'd had a taste of this country that had long eluded me and I wanted to know more, see more, experience the culture in full. I found myself often pulling out the charts and cruising guides and thinking about my next visit.

I wanted to take my time and cruise the entire north coast visiting its many deep-water bays and offshore islands. My friend Paul Sarbou, a neighbor in the Keys, jumped at the invitation to join me the following year. A veteran of Cuba travel, I had a good idea of how to provision the Peace & Plenty for the trip. We loaded canned food and dry goods, such as beans and rice. We'd have to make our own bread and Paul volunteered to be the baker, bringing a good supply of yeast and all the ingredients.

After New Year's came and went, we headed south on the same course I'd taken a year earlier. As we neared Duncan Town, Paul caught a couple of nice groupers and we dined on fresh fish in the evenings. There are few meals better than fish pulled straight from the water.

After a day in Duncan Town, we pulled anchor and set a course for Puerta de Vita, the same marina where I'd previously entered the country. The check-in process again took all morning, but we jumped through the necessary hoops and settled in for a few days.

I'd brought a large bag of used clothes to give to the people, so Paul and I walked into town, placed it on a street corner and opened it up. I told the people to take what they wanted. Within minutes, the bag was empty.

The people were so grateful. They shook our hands and thanked us for the gifts. One family invited us to their home nearby for some coffee. Once we got there, I suspected that these folks were offering us the last of their coffee ration. I tried to decline, but they would have none of it. They wanted to return the favor.

The dockmaster flagged me down when we returned to the boat that evening. He told me that I was to report to police headquarters first thing the following morning.

"Why?" I asked.

"The clothes," he told me.

This was a crime? I was furious, and a little concerned. When the dockmaster left, I began stopping everyone I could find, both Cubans and tourists. I told them my name was Chet Bright and that I'd been told to report to the police because I'd given old clothes to poor people. In case I disappeared, I wanted as many people as possible to know what had happened to me.

After a couple hours of this, the dockmaster found me again and told me to forget it. I did not have to report to the police.

The next day, we arranged for a car so we could explore the island. We visited Holguin and Santiago and found them to be beautiful, pristine towns. The countryside between Puerta de Vita and Santiago was breathtaking. We picked up hitchhikers along the way. Paul and I had studied Spanish for years and our passengers were able to point out interesting as we drove. They could also give us directions. Road signs in Cuba were scarce. If you don't know where you're going, it's easy to get lost.

Among the hitchhikers we picked up were a pair of women and their babies. We chatted with them as Paul drove along the rutted, potholed roads, which in some cases were little more than cow trails. The conversation must have been distracting because Paul drove straight into one of those vicious potholes, one wide enough for both front tires. We hit it and came to a stop. I was sure we'd lost the entire front end of the vehicle. No one was hurt, but the babies were hysterical and the mothers were trying and failing to calm them with soothing words. I climbed out of the car and was surprised to see that both front wheels remained attached. We gathered ourselves and moved on.

Winston Churchill said, "Socialism is a philosophy of failure, the creed of ignorance, and the gospel of envy, its inherent virtue is the equal sharing of misery."

I found that to be true in every inch of Cuba we traveled. Upon returning to the Peace & Plenty, we eased along the northern coast, moving east to west, and stopped at each good anchorage. The country was a marvel but the society was a shambles.

The tourist hotels were the only modern things in Cuba. They occupy prime real estate along the beautiful beaches, and unless they were employees, the locals were forbidden from venturing onto the premises. It was not uncommon to find a Cuban doctor or lawyer moonlighting at the hotels as a bartender. It paid better.

The farms on Cuba's fertile soil were government owned. The workers were paid a pittance. The tropical reefs off its coast teemed with lobsters that were illegal for the average Cuban to catch or eat. Only government-owned lobster boats were permitted.

Two months we spent in Cuba and it was an education. As they say, it's a great place to visit, but I wouldn't want to live there.

MARINA GIBSON

The islands are full of characters. Some are pleasant, some are mad, but they are unfailingly colorful. In all my years of sailing, however, few remain as strong in my memory as Mrs. Marina Gibson, proprietor of Gibson's Lunch Room on Crooked Island in the Bahamas.

Her hospitality drew me back to her small waterfront establishment many times over the years, and she was always good to me. She fed me, befriended me and even propositioned me, but I'll get to that.

I first met Mrs. Gibson and her husband in the late 1970s while en route to the Dominican Republic. The Yachtsman's Guide described Landrail Point, on the west side of Crooked Island, with such glowing language that I could not help but stop.

It painted a picture of a sun-drenched town, planted with citrus trees, and raved about the hospitality of its inhabitants, Seventh Day Adventists. Seafood and seasonal fruits and vegetables were always on sale and they had good well water and fueling operations.

I was single-handing, the kind of sailing I most enjoyed, when I pulled into a pleasant little nook off a sandy beach. I dropped the anchor, jumped into the dinghy and headed for shore and for Gibson's Lunch Room, which the Yachtsman's Guide declared was a must for visitors to Landrail Point. The place was spotless, which is not always the case in those parts.

Mr. and Mrs. Gibson gave me a warm greeting and described each item on the menu before I ordered. I had such a great experience there that after exploring the island all afternoon, I returned to Gibson's for dinner. By then, I felt I was with old friends.

The next morning I headed south, but knew that I'd be back. After a few weeks bumming around the Dominican Republic, I started making my way toward home again, traveling at my usual slow pace. On the way, I stopped once more to see the Gibsons and enjoy their hospitality.

They loaded me up with a bag of vegetables fresh out of their garden before I left for home. They wished me a safe passage.

When next I visited the following year, I was saddened to learn that not long after my last visit Mr. Gibson had taken sick and died.

Marina had no idea the cause of his illness because there were precious few doctors in those remote islands. Most people made do with home remedies and faith in God. But neither could save Mr. Gibson. He was there and he was gone without explanation.

In the meantime, Marina had kept on as always, dispensing warm island pleasantries and plates full of appetizing seafood. The lunch room had moved into the modern era in my absence. It featured a small television and VCR, a gift from a wealthy yachtsman who also supplied a box of videotapes for entertainment. Thinking that I should try to repay her kindness, I promised her that I would start sending her some tapes to watch.

She was quick to inform me that her favorite program was "I Love Lucy." So after returning home, I made sure to always record the show and mail the tapes to her.

After that, I could do no wrong and we became great friends.

On another visit, Marina confided that her daughter had married and moved with her new husband, to Liberty City, a poor and often dangerous section of Miami. She insisted then that the man was of low character and not worthy of her daughter. I discovered that her suspicions were correct months later when I got a phone call from Marina at my home in Islamorada.

Her new son-in-law had turned violent and she had flown to Miami to rescue her daughter and bring her home. But in the process, she'd run short on cash. They had money for plane tickets but not enough for anything else, not even for a bite to eat on the way home.

I told her to sit tight and I jumped in the car, drove to Miami and handed her a hundred dollars and told her she could pay me back whenever she was able.

I had no intention of ever seeing that money again, but a few months later, the mailman delivered a Bahamian money order for a hundred dollars. I took it to the post office but was told they could not cash it. Try Canada, they told me, and I did. But it came back again with a note saying that they could not help me.

In the end, I sent it back to Crooked Island and told Marina to hang onto it until I passed through again. Sure enough, the next time I walked through her door, Marina smiled that warm smile and handed me the money. She'd kept her word and that was important to her.

The Seventh-Day Adventists on Landrail Point hold to their religion and so I should not have been surprised when I dropped in to see Marina on a Saturday afternoon and she refused to cook me a hamburger.

She could not do business on the Sabbath, she said. But I also wasn't surprised when she told me that she'd just served lunch to her family and invited me to help finish off the leftover fish and vegetables. She fixed me a plate and after a few bites I put my fork down and looked at her.

"This is the best fish I've ever eaten," I said. "What is it?"

"That's barricuda," she said.

Now, one thing I'd always known sure and true is that you don't eat barricuda.

"You've poisoned me," I hollered. "I'm going to die."

Marina looked at me like I was crazy.

"Oh, no," she said. "My children had it yesterday and today, and they fine. Besides, we caught it on the north shore. They OK from there. Now if you catch them on the south shore, they poison."

As if the damn fish couldn't swim around the island. What could I do but laugh? I finished my lunch and it was indeed the best fish I've ever tasted.

Over the years, I brought many friends along on my visits to Landrail Point and I always got a kick out of their reaction when I'd walk into the lunch room, grab Marina and give her a big kiss.

Marina was never a beauty queen. But she had a heart of gold and I cared deeply for her and considered her a true friend. Once when we were having one of her wonderful meals, I was kidding her and told her that if Hazel ever left me I was going to come down to Crooked Island and marry her, get fat on her food and run the cash register.

Years later, after Hazel had passed away, I stopped in to see Marina but I'd brought with me a companion. Candy Cossuth had been a neighbor and a close friend to Hazel and me for years. Her husband had died a couple of years before Hazel did, and we were both alone and drifting like rudderless ships.

We were drawn together and enjoyed each other's company. She flew down and met me in the Dominican, intending to sail back with me to Florida. After some sightseeing there and a great sail back up to the Bahamas, Candy began having some health problems.

We decided it best if she flew back to the States to get checked out. So we stopped at Crooked Island and I asked Marina to get us some transportation to the airport. She seemed quiet, but I thought nothing of it, and she called a friend to drive us.

After dropping Candy at the airport, the friend returned me to Marina's, where I discovered the reason for her odd mood.

Once we were alone, she said to me: "You told me if anything happened to you wife, you was going to move down here. And I'm real good in bed."

Only the language she used in that last sentence wasn't quite that proper. She had taken me seriously that day when I was kidding her, and I felt very sorry about that. But she didn't stay mad for long, because when I was ready to leave she gave me what had become my usual going-away gift: Guava Duff, a cobbler made from tropical fruit that she grew in her orchard.

So we parted as friends and I enjoyed my Guava Duff all the way home.

Inside an album in my home, I keep a photo of Marina and I standing in the doorway to her lunch room, broad smiles stretched across our faces. It's been a long time since I've seen her, but I'm sure she is still cooking up that wonderful seafood and turning passing sailboaters into lifelong friends.

A MEMORABLE CRUISE

Sometimes you plan a trip and everything unfolds perfectly, the wind hits your sails and off you go, making every port stop on schedule and in the best of moods. Other times, luck and the wind are not with you.

It can be miserable. Or it can be marvelous.

In late January 1996, the Peace & Plenty left the dock with Jim Corby and my old friend Russ Swan along for a sail to the Dominican Republic. Russ is an old shipmate from my Navy years. I've known him since 1948, and I call him my old friend both because of our long friendship and because, well, he's old.

The voyage started off well enough. We loaded the boat with ample supplies and moved north to a snug little anchorage called No Name Harbor on the south end of Key Biscayne. We waited there for good weather to cross the Gulf Stream, and when our window opened, off we went, motor sailing to make good time since the Stream is no place to linger. It can get nasty and downright dangerous when you least expect it.

Once across, we anchored in behind the Gun Cay Lighthouse before crossing the Great Bahama Bank the next day on a seventy-five-mile run to the Northwest Channel Light and on to Chub Cay.

Upon the first smooth day, we made the short run to Nassau, where we lingered for several days as I visited old haunts and old friends, a grand homecoming as always.

Nassau was not our ultimate destination, so we pulled out and worked our way down the Exuma Chain, across Exuma Sound, around the north end of Long Island and down the east side to Clarence Town, another of my old favorites. I've spent many pleasant days swinging on the anchor there and was always happy to see my friend Henry Mayor, the dockmaster.

Clarence Town is one of the finest places in the Bahamas, a beautiful spot, and we planned to spend a few days taking it all in. Little did we know that it would be far more than a few days. As I said, sometimes the wind does not care about man's plans.

On our third day in Clarence Town, the breeze out of the northeast strengthened. Minute by minute, it gained intensity until it was whipping at thirty knots. We weren't going anywhere.

Winds this powerful make for a rough anchorage and to be safe, we put out a second anchor. After a couple of days, the wind still strong, an anchor line broke where it meets the chain. We put out another anchor and it happened again. This was powerful braided nylon line, but I realized that the line broke where it had been exposed to the tropical sun all summer, which had weakened the fibers. In the days that followed, the weather got worse but the line held.

The wind had been blowing strong and steady for almost two weeks and while we waited, Jim's time ran out. He had to get back to work. He caught a plane and left us floating in the breeze. That very night, I awoke to an odd feeling. The wind ... was gone. In the sudden dead calm, I yelled for Russ to wake up and get moving.

Within minutes, we were anchors up and motoring out of the harbor for points south. A weather front was passing through and when we hit open waters we found the wind had returned, but it was swinging around to the west. We raised the sails and by then the wind was blowing stronger than ever. This time, it was just as we needed. By daylight, the Peace & Plenty was breaking speed records.

By the time we reached Mayaguana, the wind had swung around to the north and we dropped anchor in Abraham's Bay, where the water was flat as a mill pond. It had been a long, strange trip and we were days from reaching the Dominican.

We worked our way down through the Turks and Caicos to Big Sand Cay. Years earlier, we'd stopped there and Russ had found a beautiful green glass fishing float. He had to go out and hunt another one. We went all over, but no luck.

Darkness was falling when we got back on the water. A nice breeze pushed us along and we set a course for Luperon on the north coast of the Dominican Republic.

Three hours later, we were making good time when the wind quit. We'd have to motor along. No problem. That is, until an hour later when the motor quit, too. This was a problem. I tried to start it again and again. Nothing.

The motor stayed dead and the wind stayed gone for two days, while we flopped and rolled and floated at the mercy of the strong westerly current. The water was too deep to drop an anchor. We were helpless and we were headed for Haiti if things didn't change.

On the third day, a light breeze sprang up. The GPS said that we were almost ready to pass the Haitian border but as we came in closer to land we were able to steer into Manzanilla Bay and worked our way up to a large ship's dock and tied up.

A Dominican navy lieutenant was in charge of the port. After checking us into the country, he had his boat crew tow us around to the anchorage in the shallow estuary outside of town and he said that he would send one of his mechanics over to look at the engine.

Once settled in, I dug around in our supplies and filled a bag with all the things I was sure he would like. Things like smoked oysters, pickled herring, pickled mushrooms and other gourmet goodies. I presented him with the bag and after that I could do no wrong. I had made a friend and he turned out to be a good one.

The place was Pepillo Salcedo, and it is the westernmost town on the north shore of Dominican, a short distance from the Haitian border. An American fruit company had moved in during the time the Dominican was ruled by Rafael Trujillo. His reign was often a violent one but his opposition to communism made for warm relations with the United States.

The company paid to clear out the jungle and built the town of Pepillo Salcedo to house its workers. The streets were laid out, and neat little brick houses were built, along with a massive dock for their ships to load bananas. After Trujillo's assassination in 1961, the fruit company pulled out and left behind a beautiful town full of people with no a means to make a living. But they survived. It was no longer a thriving place, but maybe that was the beauty of it.

Russ had been away from home too long by his estimation and wanted to get back, so he caught a bus for Santo Domingo and the airport, leaving me on my own in a town where, best I could tell, two people spoke English.

After a few days, the mechanic came by and checked out the engine. The injectors needed overhauling. He carried them to his repair shop and brought them back later as good as new. With all my problems solved, and in no particular hurry, I started to get to know the town. Most of my days were taken up with shopping. The people there had an interesting way of doing business.

If I wanted chicken for dinner, I made my way to the chicken house, walked in and asked for a chicken.

"Muerto o vivo?" came the response. Dead or alive?

"Muerto," I'd say, and the proprietor would kill and clean the chicken right there on the spot.

If I wanted red meat, I strolled over to the carniceria, the meat market, which consisted of little more than a sturdy tree outside of town. One day the butcher would have a calf hanging in the tree. The next day it might be a lamb or a goat or a pig. All I had to do was point out the cut of meat I wanted. It was wise, however, to get there early in the morning because there was no refrigeration at the meat market. Show up early and bring the cooler.

The cooler turned out to be necessary because on the road that led back to the boat I discovered the finest bar in town. An outdoor establishment with tables set up beneath a giant tree that shaded a vast swath of the ground beneath it.

The proprietor knew how to keep customers like me happy because when I arrived, he'd take my cooler full of meat and dump ice into it, ensuring I'd be in no rush to get back to the boat. I've never found a beer I enjoyed as much as the Dominican-brewed Presidente Beer. I passed many an hour beneath that shade tree, just me and my Presidente.

On Saturday nights in Pepillo Salcedo the air is sweet with the smells of barbecuing chicken and ribs. The residents set up their cookers in the front yards and as the flames rise, neighbors walk the street, stopping and strolling into the yards to buy the grilled meats for their families.

And then you hear it. The notes rise into the air, merengue music emanating from the town's dance hall. As the hour grows later on Saturday night, the entire town flocks to the dance hall. Men, women and children, entranced by the island rhythms. For an outsider, there is nothing to do but join in.

On the night I left Pepillo Salcedo, the music enveloped the town. I sailed through the estuary, lamenting that I'd discovered this place so late in life, what I now believe to be the best the Dominican has to offer.

I passed the dance hall, and a friend on the shore bid me farewell with a thumbs up. As I moved into Manzanilla Bay, heading north, the notes faded away and the wonderful merengue beat went silent.

SWALLOWING THE ANCHOR

For the better part of seven decades, the sea dominated my life. It carried me around the world, in times of war and times of peace. It has terrified me and it has thrilled me. I've ridden its waves and dived its depths. I've come to know it intimately in its many mercurial moods and, all things considered, it's been very good to me.

But as I've aged, my body has grown weaker and so too has my mind. In recent years, I came to the realization that I no longer could cope with the sea's unpredictability, and I knew that if I ignored this, sooner or later, I'd find trouble. Or it would find me.

Sailors call it "swallowing the anchor." It signifies moving ashore and giving up the sea as a way of life, draining the saltwater from your veins.

I swallowed the anchor in the summer of 2009, weeks shy of my eighty-fourth birthday.

The open waters were not a safe place for me anymore, but the Peace & Plenty remained as capable as ever. I had to find a new home for her, and it was an easy decision. My daughter Andie and her husband, Jim, have a beautiful home on Cobb Island, overlooking the Potomac River in Maryland, a few miles from the Chesapeake Bay and a short distance from the very spot that we launched the Peace &

Plenty thirty-seven years earlier, in 1972. I decided that the Peace & Plenty should remain in the family and in familiar waters.

Their oldest son, Brent, lives in Richmond, Virginia, not far from Andie and Jim. He was the perfect choice to become the new captain. He's always loved the sea and the outdoors, and it is some solace to me to think about the wonderful days that lay ahead for Brent and his family aboard the boat that has brought me so many wonderful memories.

But handing over the wheel required one last journey. Jim had made many trips with me to the islands and was a great shipmate. He traveled to Florida late that summer to help sail her up to Intracoastal Waterway to Maryland. The trip would last about three weeks.

There was no reason to load heavy with supplies since we could stop at many places along the way. With minimal preparation we sailed north. About the only time we stopped at a marina was when we needed fuel. With the price they ask for an overnight slip, you have to have a very low regard for your money to consider it. It's much more peaceful out on the anchor, and there are many good anchorages along the waterway.

Perfect weather welcomed us on the opening leg of the trip. We motor sailed all the way, taking turns at the wheel. When the wind was strong, we unfurled the jib to help us along.

Of course, it wouldn't be right if the trip didn't include a few misadventures. The first came near Fernandina Beach, south of the Georgia line. We'd planned to spend the night there off the main channel. As you approach, the waterway twists and turns and a sailor must be ever vigilant. Jim was at the wheel and working his way through, when I heard him speak up.

"It looks like that boat up ahead is aground," he said.

The words no sooner left his mouth than we heard an unmistakable noise beneath us. We had run aground, too.

We managed to back off without much trouble and moved on to our anchorage, but it was a fitting little hiccup, given that Hazel and I had run aground when we first took the Peace & Plenty down the Intracoastal during our move to the Keys.

We made it a point to spend the night in Beaufort, South Carolina, one of the prettiest towns on the waterway and one that Jim and Andie visit at every opportunity. But continuing north, we didn't get far before Mother Nature stepped in and added another bit of symmetry to our journey. By the time that we crossed North Carolina's Cape Fear River, weather reports were sounding ominous. High winds were coming, so we broke our own rule and headed for a marina.

We chose the Carolina Beach State Park, which has a fifty-four-slip marina and offers good protection. It is the same marina where we worked from during our dives on Civil War blockade runners in the early 1960s.

Jim and I barely had time to get lines to the dock when the winds began to roar and the rain came down in buckets. Three days it kept coming down and three days we waited for our chance to move on. But it was a snug little marina and the people who ran it were typical North Carolina people, friendly and warm and willing to do just about anything for you. They always make you feel at home.

After a few more days, we passed Norfolk, Virginia, and headed north on the Chesapeake Bay. We were back in familiar waters, working our way up to the Potomac River and then upstream a few miles to spend the night at Tall Timbers, where the Peace & Plenty, with Jim and I aboard, had spent her first night at anchor after we launched her in 1972. We both had fond memories of Tall Timbers and it was, all these years later, the perfect spot.

The following day, on our way up the river, I dressed the old girl with the courtesy flags of all of the foreign countries that she had carried me to through the years. What a picture she made with all those bright-colored flags streaming in the breeze.

A lump found its way to my throat and tears welled up in my eyes as I looked out over those banners and reminisced about all the years and all the miles.

Hard to believe it was coming to an end, but it was a fitting end.

As we guided the boat toward its new home in a small marina on Cobb Island, little by little we caught sight of Andie and her sister Sandie waiting on the dock with a bottle of champagne.

It had been nearly seventy years since I stood on the pier in Norfolk, looked out over the ocean and stepped aboard the Navy troopship. Now, from the deck of the Peace & Plenty, I surveyed the water once more, and then stepped off onto the dock.

My daughters welcomed me with hugs and kisses and smiles. We popped the champagne and toasted the end of an amazing journey.

My Heart's at Sea Forever

Long ago I was a Sailor.
I sailed the Ocean blue.
I knew the bars in Singapore...
The coastline of Peru.
I knew well the sting of salt spray,
The taste of Spanish wine,
The beauty of the Orient...
Yes, all these things were mine.
But I wear a different hat now,
No tie and jacket too.
My sailing days were long ago...
with that life I am through.
But somewhere deep inside of me...
The sailor lives there still.
He longs to go to sea again,
But knows he never will.
My love, my life, is here at home,
and I will leave here never.
Though mind and body stay ashore...
My heart's at sea forever.

Author Unknown

ABOUT THE AUTHORS

Chet Bright is a retired senior chief petty officer and a veteran of World War II and the Korean War, where he was a member of the Navy's elite Underwater Demolition Teams. He is a former instructor at the Navy's Explosive Ordnance Disposal School and served in Vietnam with the National Oceanographic Office. In retirement, he captained the Peace & Plenty for nearly 40 years. He lives in Stuart, Florida.

Derek Turner is the Washington Bureau Chief for Stars and Stripes, the independent newspaper serving the U.S. military around the world. He lives in La Plata, Maryland.